BURN DOWN THE CASTLE

BURN DOWN THE CASTLE

A PLANNING MODEL FOR SMALL TEAMS

DAVID MAIDMENT

Character illustrations © 2023 Shelley Weston.

Paperback ISBN: 978-1-7394137-0-5.

Hardcover ISBN: 978-1-7394137-1-2.

Published by Scripta Scripta.

For those who don't mind starting again

CONTENTS

Preface   xi

THE PARABLE

1. AN EXCITING PARTNERSHIP   3
2. TWO WEEKS EARLIER   5
3. IN THE CROSSHAIRS   11
4. REGARDING THE NEW PROJECT...   17
5. DISASTER ONE MONTH IN   21
6. DEEP INSIDE THE BLACK BOX   25
7. A CLASSIC LIVE DEMO   29
8. PASSING THE BUCK   35
9. DEAR DRU   37
10. HALF A PIANO   39
11. THE FALLOUT   43
12. SOME HARSH TRUTHS   47
13. A HIDDEN SKILL   51
14. A DIFFERENT APPROACH   59
15. RALLYING THE TROOPS   65
16. THE NEW WORK IN PROGRESS   73
17. DEMO 2.0   75
18. PREPARING TO LAUNCH   81
19. THE MOMENT OF TRUTH   87
    EPILOGUE   93

UNDERSTANDING THE MODEL

OVERVIEW   99

MISSION CRITICAL   103
Building what is obvious   104
Learning from the past   106
Understanding the problem   107
Challenging assumptions   108
Burning down the castle   111

STROKE OF GENIUS   115

Having a wonderful insight   116
Being ahead of your time   117
Not understanding the users' requirements   120
One step at a time   121
Dogfooding to test your hypotheses   124
Checking your assumptions   124

VISION ≠ REALITY   127
Building according to plan   128
Forgetting what is important   130
Optimising for the future   131
Building for the wrong audience   133
Revisiting past projects   135

WASTE OF TIME   137
Exploring a Stroke of Genius   137
Chasing shiny things   138
Idealised building   141
Culling an idea if in doubt   141
It doesn't count if the problem isn't solved   142
Digging yourself out of a hole   142
Realigning against the original problem   145

IMPLEMENTING THE MODEL

APPLYING PREEMPTIVELY   149
Building the essential   150
Taking a chance   157
Getting back on track   162
Burning down the castle   167

CHECKLISTS FOR APPLYING PREEMPTIVELY   175
Mission critical   176
Stroke of genius   177
Vision ≠ reality   178
Waste of time   179

APPLYING RETROSPECTIVELY   181
Validating proof of concepts   181
Evaluating your execution   182
Benchmarking an entire product   183
Finding bottlenecks   186

FINAL THOUGHTS

HOW THE MODEL FITS IN	191
THE JOB VERSUS THE SOLUTION	193
BUILD, MEASURE, ITERATE; ALWAYS	195
AIM TO SUCCEED OR FAIL	197
COMMON SENSE SHOULD PREVAIL	199
DON'T BE AFRAID TO MAKE TOUGH CHOICES	201
Glossary	203
Acknowledgements	211
About the author	212
Also by David Maidment	213

PREFACE

I have been a software developer for most of my life.

One of my earliest memories of creating a piece of software is sitting down in front of an IBM personal computer with a 5¼-inch floppy disk drive and severe screen burn-in, and figuring out how to emit a siren waveform through the onboard speaker.

Whether the enjoyment of that moment came from creating something from scratch, or from annoying my family, I cannot be sure. But one thing I *am* sure of is that I had no inkling that people might one day pay good money for such shenanigans.

So for many years, coding was a fun pastime and nothing more.

If I needed a piece of software, I would sooner build it than buy it. As a teenager, I listened to music with my own media centre, edited photos with my own graphics tools, kept notes with my own word processor, and made my old Windows 3.1 system look and feel more like Windows 95 with Start Menu and Explorer programs.

All of which is to say that from a very early age, I have been writing software that I *knew* solved a problem, because the problem almost always belonged to me.

This trend continued into my professional life.

Still unaware that *software development* was even possible as a career, I landed in the world of retail, where I quickly began to write software to automate the boring parts of my job. What I thought was a cheeky way for myself and my colleagues to effectively bunk off by doing less work, turned out to be a thorough digital transformation for the business—not that I realised that's what I was doing at the time.

But when I took that success, moved to a large city, and took on 'proper' software jobs, things changed.

Working on client projects meant that, for the first time in my life, the Venn diagram that represented myself and the end user was not one circle stacked neatly on top of another.

Call it imposter syndrome, but I began to doubt my work. A question that would rear its head early and often was: *Will anyone use this?*

Sometimes that fear turned out to be prophetic. There have

been complex software systems with hard, unmovable deadlines that no one even attempted to log into for six months after launch.

And, much to my surprise, there have also been small, throwaway tools that have reduced months of work to a few clicks, and have been praised as veritable game changers.

And if you had asked me beforehand which project would fall into which category, I would have guessed wrong most of the time.

As I have taken on more senior roles in my career, and have worked more closely with Product and User Experience (UX) people, I have thought more about what makes for a successful project. Reflecting on the projects that have gone well and those that have not, it is undeniable that those that enjoyed the highest levels of use and solved problems the most thoroughly were those where the core problem was most clearly understood.

It turns out that the least successful projects have tended to be those where assumptions were made, and the most successful projects were those where assumptions were *not* made.

Specifically: in successful projects, we did not assume that, if someone told us they *wanted* something, they actually *needed* it; we did not assume that all of the right people had been involved in the planning process just because a product specification had been produced; and we did not assume that we actually understood the problem just because someone had explained it to us.

I began to crystallise this thinking in early 2021, when I was asked to write a few articles for a group of local CTOs. In one article, entitled *Should you build it, or abandon it?*, I thought of ways to illustrate the thinking that had led most of the successful and unsuccessful projects in my life, and came up with the following diagram:

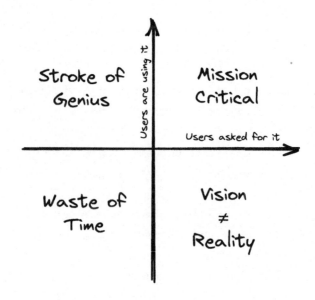

It essentially asks two simple questions:

1. Are we building something users need?
2. Will it see use?

When you dig down into each of those questions, some interesting thoughts occur.

The first question may be better understood as, *Is what we're building solving a problem the user has?* This raises all kinds of further questions around your interaction with the user, the work they are doing, the problems they are experiencing, and how well anyone involved actually understands those problems.

The second question prompts further questions about the extent to which your solution is being used (or, if still in development, whether it *will* be used), how well you have built it, how easy it is to use, whether it is openly embraced or grudgingly accepted, and whether it solves the entirety of the problem or only a part of it.

The labels assigned to each quadrant of the grid provide a

neat—if not oversimplified—way of thinking about the products and features (hereafter referred to as *solutions*) that fall into them.

You may choose to assign a solution 1:1 to a quadrant by answering the two questions in a binary *yes/no* fashion, or you may find more value in plotting them on a sliding scale and positioning them more precisely within a quadrant. The latter can prove useful if you are comparing multiple solutions against each other.

The ideal state for a solution is to land in the top-right quadrant of the grid, the so-called Mission Critical state. But it can be just as useful to focus on the other quadrants, where disruptive ideas and cautionary tales reside. The title of this book, *Burn Down The Castle*, refers to the fact that it can actually be a good thing to identify something as a Waste of Time and quit while you are ahead, no matter how much time has been spent on the ill-advised solution to date.

The article I ended up writing in support of this model was long enough to get across the general point, but too short to delve into the multitude of edge cases that really make it interesting.

This book is, therefore, an extension of that article. Its intended audience is those who work in tech (or tech-supported) companies that do not have at least one dedicated product owner; where everyone—software developers, salespeople, the CEO—regularly has to make decisions about how the product should be built.

It begins with a parable; a story of an average development team making all of the usual mistakes, pushed close to disaster, and rescued by someone who has the bravery to ask tough questions about a failing project.

All of the parable's characters are flawed in some way—there are no real heroes or villains; just a group of humans who are trying to solve a problem.

If stories are not your thing, you can begin reading about the model in more depth roughly halfway through this book, and fill in the gaps from context.

Although the narrative of the parable only explores a thin slice of the model, it does touch on many of the topics on which the book later elaborates. In the parable you may recognise characters, situations, and conversations from your own career, which you can then follow to their logical conclusion with the help of the latter half of the book.

Finally, it is important when reading this book to think of the model merely as a trick to add to your arsenal, to use alongside other methods and tools. It should not make binary decisions for you, but should force you to ask the questions that prompt a deeper understanding of what you are building and why. Then you can make the tough decisions.

THE PARABLE

CHAPTER 1
AN EXCITING PARTNERSHIP

 CamelCat Marketing Partners with Owliphant Insights for New Machine Learning Venture

Ethical marketing experts CamelCat Marketing have partnered with venture-backed machine learning startup Owliphant Insights to expand their CRM offering.

Owliphant Insights's cutting-edge *ML-Cast* technology will be incorporated into CamelCat Marketing's state-of-the-art platform to enable marketers to position more highly relevant products and offers before existing customers than has traditionally been possible with off-the-shelf marketing tools.

The partnership marks an exciting move for CamelCat Marketing into the burgeoning machine learning space.

CHAPTER 2
TWO WEEKS EARLIER

'IT'S WILD—I know three devs who reneged on roles just before they started because they got better offers. One was double the money!'

'Their boss counter-offered double the salary?'

'No; it was one of the other places they interviewed. They'd turned them down, accepted with some other company, then the first place shoved a bunch of cash in their face. It's *mad* right now. I have a friend, Charlie, who's been trying to hire for six months, but can't find anyone good because the market's so hot. She can't move fast enough to get anyone.'

Charlie's friend was Evelyn, a senior developer at CamelCat Marketing. She was speaking to James, one of the company's mid-level developers. Sat in a meeting room with the rest of the development team, they chatted while waiting for their CTO, Cameron.

CamelCat Marketing was a small, bootstrapped marketing agency that had found its niche in providing *ethical marketing for clients who care*. What *exactly* that meant was not widely understood in the team. But they were software developers; they were in the tech industry, not the marketing industry.

Evelyn had been with the company the longest. She was a front-end developer who enjoyed learning new things. Her whole career had been spent in agencies, working on projects for small-to-medium-sized clients. It was repetitive work, but the repetition provided opportunities to hone her art.

James wasn't yet battle-worn. He had dabbled in front-end work under Evelyn and Robert, back-end work under Cameron, and informally mentored the team's junior developer, Kyle, but he hadn't yet decided where to specialise.

'So why aren't we all out earning the big bucks?' he asked.

Robert glanced toward Kyle. It was a valid question, but he didn't want to fill juniors' heads with lofty ideas about the grass always being greener. In his experience there were weeds everywhere.

It was difficult to know what Kyle thought of such talk. He was very young, and very keen. He had been described as a 'sponge', and with good reason. He soaked up knowledge, and delighted in learning. Evelyn had secretly taken bets on how long it would take for him to become jaded like every other developer she knew.

She answered James's question by asking one of her own: 'I don't know. Why aren't you?'

Most of the team laughed.

'Touché,' said James, tipping an imaginary hat.

Then she answered seriously: 'For real, though, it's a lot of fucking about finding a new job. And things here aren't terrible. I considered moonlighting for that friend I mentioned, to help her out, but I'm too lazy. Or not enough of a masochist. I have no idea how Rob does all those side projects and stays sane.'

It was true. Robert took on a steady stream of side projects. And he earned well from them—anyone who paid attention to the various gadgets he had delivered to the office could tell that. But how he managed to effectively work two jobs was not clear. Maybe it was his love for what he did? After all, he only took on jobs—whether side projects or day jobs—that aligned with his values.

As the conversation continued, Cameron strode into the room.

Cameron was not only the company's CTO, but also one of its founders, and a veteran coder. He was endlessly interested in figuring out the guts of things. He also had a certain ease about him. He waltzed into every room, often late, but always bearing gifts. On this occasion he brought doughnuts, which he slid onto the large table around which his team were sat.

'Doughnuts up!' he proclaimed.

Everyone scrambled for the doughnuts with the best toppings. Why the doughnut company bothered making the plain ones was a mystery.

As they snacked, Cameron set up his laptop. A large television stood at the head of the table, which he plugged into. He then sat down and kicked off the meeting, a combination of sprint planning and retrospective.

The meeting was largely uneventful: Robert and Evelyn had finished reskinning a landing page, which was with the client for sign-off; Alice had been on rotation picking up support tickets; Kyle had been shadowing Alice; and James had completed half of a much-needed revamp of the CamelCat Marketing website. The upcoming sprint was filled with much the same kind of work. With a click of a button it started, and the meeting ended.

As the team shuffled out of the room, Cameron called for Evelyn and Robert to remain.

They stood by the table, waiting for a good 30 seconds before Cameron finished whatever he was doing and looked up at them. He smiled, as if to greet them for the first time that day.

'Please, sit!' he instructed.

Robert leant on the table. 'Do we need our laptops, or…?'

Cameron shook his head. He closed his laptop and leant forward. 'What do you both think about doing some machine learning?' he asked.

It was not something Robert had given a tremendous amount of thought to. Like most developers he had dabbled with free trials from cloud providers, but purely as a curiosity, and not recently.

'Do we have a new project?' he asked.

Cameron smiled, springing up from his chair. 'We do!' he exclaimed. 'PB want us to build a new dashboard. It's going to do all kinds of cool things. And it'll be powered by ML.'

PB referred to *Purple Budgie Finance*, an online broker and advisory service. They were also CamelCat Marketing's largest client, accounting for somewhere in the region of 40% of their recurring revenue. When they said, *Jump!*, the only correct response was, *How high?*

Evelyn leaned in. She had a keen interest in machine

learning. The last two conferences she attended had excellent machine learning tracks. She attended as many of the sessions as she could—the boring talks about backbone latencies and observability tooling could go do one; she wanted to hear how real companies solved complex problems at scale.

'What kind of things?' she asked.

Cameron was happy to elaborate: 'We need to build a recommendation algorithm, for one. They want to slice up their customers and figure out opportunities to cross-sell.'

Evelyn suppressed a snicker. The thought of slicing up customers was an appealing one. When Cameron's attention turned to her she put on her most grown-up voice and said, 'Go on.'

Cameron shrugged. The joke hadn't landed. He continued: 'If you think about it, they have loads of data. All the advice they give, products they sell, policies redeemed... even the sales that don't convert. And if a streaming service can tell me what I should watch next, there's no reason PB can't make just-as-insightful recommendations to their customers.'

Robert had been listening intently. He was not one to get carried away with hype; he had some questions.

'Is this something we're set up to do? And what about the mission statement? We're all about ethical marketing. This sounds kind of spammy.'

He stopped short of parroting the corporate slogan—*ethical marketing for clients who care*—but the words lingered in the air as though he *had* spoken them.

He fell silent. He had two simple, direct questions, and awaited their answer.

Cameron was no stranger to Robert toeing the company line. It was part of the reason Dru, the company's CEO and co-founder, had insisted on hiring him. As a developer he was fairly talented, but people who really *got* the company were a rare breed. Or so Dru said. Cameron was just responsible for the tech.

Before Cameron could answer, Evelyn stepped in to reframe Robert's first question: 'More to the point: where is all this ML coming from?' She drew from her mental conference notes. 'Because our cloud provider's offering is a bit… shit. Are we going multicloud?' Assuming that the answer must be *yes*, she then asked, 'Will we have problems passing the data back and forth at scale?'

Those missed talks about backbone latencies might have been useful after all.

'Don't worry, I've got it covered,' Cameron reassured her. 'I've got some demos lined-up. There's this one startup doing really cool things with machine learning that I'm meeting with this week. Just leave all the complicated stuff to me, and get cracking on the front end. I'll have more details next week.'

'You want us to start on the front end now?' Robert asked.

So much for the two weeks worth of work they had just finished planning.

Cameron nodded. 'Yep. Just spin up our standard dashboard template. Admin panel, user roles… you know the drill. I'll kick a few wireframes over to you the next few days for what I think the other pages will need to look like. I reckon by the end of next week we can have a POC of some basic features. So let's get started. Chop chop!'

CHAPTER 3
IN THE CROSSHAIRS

At 8:20 a.m. on Monday morning, Julie arrived in the office to find Cameron and Dru already working. This was not uncommon—Dru was a workaholic and Cameron was liable to show up at any hour of the day. Keen to get the most out of her internship, Julie often joined them; it was the best time of the day to get Dru's undivided attention and learn something real about marketing.

What was not common was for Cameron to talk to her.

But talk he did. With Dru busy on a phone call, Julie was lost for something to do, so Cameron took advantage of a captive audience. He began a lengthy exposition on the exciting machine learning tech he had settled on, going into the ins and the outs, the benefits and the pitfalls.

She humoured him with affirming noises and nods of the head, but when Cameron realised after twenty minutes that the conversation was one-sided, he gave up. Julie's inability to upskill on a brand new and complex topic outside her area of expertise, in real time, did her no favours with Cameron.

Just before things became awkward, the development team

filtered noisily into the office. Cameron collared them to begin his exposition anew.

He showcased the platform they would use to power Purple Budgie Finance's new recommendation engine and spoke passionately about how proud they should be to work for such a forward-thinking company. They were going to change the world in some small way. All thanks to his eye for innovation and Dru's acceptance of his eye for innovation.

Dru was still in her office, engaged in an increasingly animated phone conversation. She leant over her desk, her chair pushed back, her hands curled into fists, and her usually serene demeanour nowhere to be found. The phone receiver was cast upon the desk, and the conversation had transitioned to loud speaker.

Whatever had been said, Dru was incensed.

'I can't believe you're blaming *my* team for *your* ads!'

The person laying the blame at Dru's feet was Oscar, Purple

Budgie Finance's Head of Sales. He was the driving force behind the new machine learning project, and had commissioned many tools and services from CamelCat Marketing over the years. So when something went wrong, he was the one calling to complain.

The last piece of work his company had commissioned was an advertising campaign. And it had not been well-received.

'The backlash on social media over the weekend was unacceptable!' he barked. 'Our CEO is furious. How you could create something so tone-deaf is beyond me.'

But Dru was not having it. She knew exactly why the campaign had backfired, as did everyone else who worked on it. They had all warned him. She would not be taking the blame.

'No. No! I warned you about those ads. I told you *exactly* what would happen. But you insisted we make them anyway. "No deviation from the spec," you said. My team couldn't have been more clear that it'd blow up in your face!'

Oscar skirted around the subject of his culpability. 'The fact remains. Our budgets are being slashed so we're reassessing vendors. Keeping you guys on the books will be a hard sell after this fuckup. You're lucky Accelerate was already signed off. Knock it out the park and maybe you'll get lucky.'

Accelerate was the codename for Cameron's new machine learning project. What had started the day as a run-of-the-mill project was now the most important project they would ever work on.

No pressure, then.

A few more pointed words were exchanged and Dru slammed the receiver down. Oscar had already hung up, of course. The power dynamic had shifted such that she knew to tread just a little bit more carefully.

But it didn't make her any less angry.

Her hands were shaking. Yes, her team had worked on tone-deaf adverts that had offended a lot of people, but their numerous warnings had been ignored. *If the company survives long enough to get new clients*, she told herself, *I'll establish tougher ground rules on what is acceptable.*

She breathed deeply and counted to ten, then cracked open the door and called for Cameron.

He sauntered into her office.

'What's up?' he asked. 'Who was on the phone? Delivery company lose your parcel again?'

This was not a time for levity.

'That was Oscar,' Dru explained.

'PB? What'd he want?'

'It seems they're reassessing their contracts.'

That was certainly a delicate way to put it.

'So… more money?' Cameron joked.

Dru shook her head and elaborated: 'Quite the opposite. The backlash from those awful ads has landed on us. So Accelerate might be the last piece of work we do for them. Unless we "knock it out the park".'

She made air quotes as she repeated Oscar's words.

Cameron considered the situation for a moment.

'Fuck 'em,' he concluded. 'We have other clients.'

Dru could not believe what she was hearing. Could a person so smart really be *that* dense? Surely he could connect the dots?

'Cam, they make up almost half our revenue. I…' She was literally lost for words. 'They're a crappy client, but if we lose them, that's it. Game over. CamelCat Marketing disappears and we have to get regular jobs.'

'Speak for yourself,' Cameron said, cocking an eyebrow. 'The city's crying out for CTOs like me.'

Dru's hands once more began to shake. All of her anger at Oscar resurfaced, focused now on the man stood before her, the one person who *should* be on her side and looking out for their company.

'Damn it Cameron, don't you care about this thing we've built? All the late nights; all the sacrifices?' She pointed out towards their employees, blissfully working away. 'About them?'

Cameron waved away her concerns.

'Dru, chill. Accelerate's going great. We'll probably even ship ahead of the deadline. I've got the ML vendor lined up, so we can put out a press release. All that's left is the boring task of stitching it all together. Oscar's full of shit, anyway; ten quid says he's blagging.'

Cameron may have been right about Oscar's threat. But the stakes were too high to call his bluff. The project had to succeed beyond expectations, and they had to secure more work for the following quarter. Then they had to win more clients to diversify their risk.

CHAPTER 4
REGARDING THE NEW PROJECT...

AS A TECH-ENABLED COMPANY, CamelCat Marketing was mostly staffed by twenty-somethings. And on-trend, most of those twenty-somethings called the city centre 'home'. Near the cafés, the pubs, the museums, the nightlife... the whole never-ending experience of *being* in the city.

It was an understandable allure, but not one that had caught Robert. Married early, with strong family ties, and the possibility of a family of his own in the near future, Suburbia was the only place it made sense to put down roots.

Suburbia was also Cameron's home. He had been lucky enough to inherit a bungalow from his grandmother, and seemed content to forego the hustle and bustle so loved by his peers.

They both lived the same side of town, and were served by the same train line. Whenever they both managed to finish work on time, they would share the walk to the train station, and then a train journey most of the way home.

On the day Purple Budgie Finance had threatened CamelCat Marketing's existence, Robert had something on his mind. He timed his departure to match Cameron's so he could get him alone and talk shop.

Their topics of conversation were often filler: what video games they were playing, recent announcements from tech conferences, the latest football upset. Work was not usually on the cards. So when, several minutes into their walk, they came to a stop at a busy crossing, Robert dove in.

'Is this project really us?' he asked. 'I know I must sound like a broken record, but we're supposed to be the good guys in marketing. And this new project is straight-up Marketing 101: sell something to someone, then do whatever it takes to sell them something else.'

He glanced around. It was dark already, and starting to get cold. As he sighed, his breath hung in the air. It was a good thing the train station was so close.

Cameron did not respond.

They navigated the crossing.

Did he even hear me? Robert wondered.

He then tried a different tack: 'Look, to be blunt, I left my last place because they had us building projects like this. And I came to work *here* because of our brand values. Maybe I'm asking a lot from a marketing company, but I'm genuinely worried this is a slippery slope that leads further and further away from what we stand for.'

Eventually, Cameron turned to Robert and threw up his hands, offering a shrug.

'You know, Rob, I get it, but sometimes you just can't be so principled. There's a project that's landed on our desk, it's a big one, and it lets us use some really cool tech. There will be plenty of other projects that are more *you*, so just suck this one up, you know? And if it helps you sleep at night, I'm doing all the tricky bits anyway; your front-end work's neither good nor evil, you know?'

That was certainly *one* way to deflect from the real conversation.

Cameron tilted his head back, opened his mouth and exhaled heavily. A stream of mist poured out of his mouth and into the chilly air. He puckered his lips and repeated the action a few more times, playing as if he were blowing smoke rings.

'I love this time of year!' he exclaimed. 'Are you and the missus going away for Christmas again?'

But Robert wasn't going to be sucked into a nonsense conversation. Nor was he satisfied that their previous conversation had reached an acceptable conclusion.

'No, we're staying home,' he said, before trying one more time: 'Listen, Cam, I'm just worried about our approach. ML doesn't have a great track record of being fair, you know? Don't get me wrong, I love it as a concept, but you're talking about a magic black box that we can't explain the inner workings of. One of our company values is *Transparency*; how do we square that with letting some machine decide how to manipulate people into spending money they didn't want to?'

'Is that what you think we do?!' Cameron questioned.

Robert was taken aback. *Of course that was what they were doing*. But more so he was surprised by his boss's reaction.

Cameron did not wait for an answer. As they entered the train station, he strode ahead, shaking his head and muttering something to himself.

Maybe he does *care about what we do?* Robert wondered, marvelling at the brief flash of moral outrage he had just witnessed. *But then why do we build shit like this? And that god-awful spreadsheet-in-a-browser project last year? And all the others?*

CHAPTER 5
DISASTER ONE MONTH IN

CAMERON WASN'T the biggest fan of Dru's office. In an open-plan work environment, one walled-off corner—and a transparent one, at that!—just looked kind of weird. It didn't quite evoke the image of a strict schoolmarm watching over the children, but there was *something* going on along those lines. Maybe a spy chief looking down on the worker bees that would soon be sent on a one-way mission deep into enemy territory, liable to defect the moment they landed?

In any event, when he found himself summoned to her office, it was an unwelcome start to the day. And he could tell by the look on her face that she had not called him in for a coffee and a friendly chat.

So much for coding this morning, he thought. *Maybe I can carry on in my mind's IDE.*

He sat down in the chair across from her and settled in for the long haul, leaning back and putting his feet up on the PC tower that protruded from beneath Dru's desk. Officially, it was the internal NAS, where work was backed up at the end of each day. But unofficially, it was where everyone shared whatever films they had recently pirated.

Dru glanced at his feet. Her eyes narrowed somewhat.

'You know why I wanted to talk, right?' she asked.

Cameron shrugged. In his head he replayed various things she could have been upset about, before settling on the most recent. 'Is it about Owliphant?'

Dru exhaled loudly. 'Yes, Cam, it's about Owliphant.'

Internally, Cameron sighed in relief.

'Jesus, Dru, don't scare me. I thought I'd broken your favourite LP again or something.'

Dru stood on the other side of the desk. She leaned over and looked him dead in the eye. She wasn't joking.

'First of all,' she said, 'you still owe me for that record. Second, do you not get what a big deal this is?'

'It'll blow over,' Cameron reassured her.

It *would* blow over, right? People had increasingly short attention spans nowadays.

'Please tell me you understand it's not about that.' She looked like she would have shook him, were there not a desk between them. 'Cam, please. It's not about whether it'll blow over. It's about our reputation, and how fucked this makes us.'

Dru was dealing with the fallout from Owliphant Insights shutting up shop after their supposedly revolutionary ML and AI tools had been shown to exhibit troubling biases against minorities. It had not been long since CamelCat Marketing put out a press release aligning themselves with the technology, and now the heat was on.

'I thought you put out comms distancing us from the scandal?' Cameron asked.

Dru slumped down in her chair. 'We did. But it's a matter of perception. People will wonder how we could have made such a poor choice. If we were anyone else, maybe we'd get a pass, but we're ethical marketers. It's in our corporate values. It's all over our website... It's the thing I go into schools and talk to kids about. This is going to stick. And on top of that, I doubt we can finish our project without the tech, so the company will probably go bust, too.'

'Hey, don't worry about it,' Cameron sought to reassure her. 'I've already started working on my own version of the tech. It's quite easy, really. A few evenings and weekends from me and we'll be back on track. Forget those Owliphant jokers; they had no business running a tech company.'

Dru shook her head. 'I still can't believe how awful that exposé was. I mean, how does that even happen?'

A smile spread across Cameron's face. He raised his hand

slightly, extending his index finger to catch her attention. An opportunity to explain something clever to the civilians around him! He lived for such moments.

'Well…'

Dru looked up and caught the oncoming exposition. She leaned fully across the desk and swatted his hand down. Her frustration, which had turned into dejection, now turned into anger.

'I swear to God, if you start explaining training biases to me, I'll lose it.'

Maybe now wasn't the time to show off. No worries; the rewrite wouldn't take long—he'd blow her mind later. Their next press release would be something to write home about. They'd soon be the tech company every developer within a hundred-mile radius wanted to work for.

Cameron kicked off from the PC tower, swivelling around in the chair and launching into an effortless waltz out the door.

'Don't worry about a thing,' he called back to Dru. 'This time next month, we'll be laughing.'

As the door closed behind him, Dru could be heard grumbling to herself. But it was fine; she worried too much, anyway.

One person who had picked up on Dru's grumbling was Alice, who looked up from her desk to catch Dru's gaze. She observed her for a few seconds, then turned back to her desk and scribbled something into her notebook.

CHAPTER 6
DEEP INSIDE THE BLACK BOX

TRUE TO HIS WORD, Cameron was putting in the hours to get his ML-Cast replacement across the line. But it had not taken the few evenings and weekends he had predicted—it had quickly turned into *every* evening and weekend.

To accommodate the additional work, his working hours had shifted. He would appear in the office mid-afternoon, work late into the night and catch the last train home. When he was so engrossed in his work that he missed that train, it was not uncommon for the team to find him asleep on one of the office's sofas the following morning. Sometimes there was cold pizza in the kitchenette.

When his working hours overlapped with others, he was notable by his spotty attendance in meetings. 1:1s with the developers had gone completely out the window, and on the rare occasion he joined the others for a meeting, it was usually because he was already occupying the meeting room and the meeting just happened around him.

The mornings that he was absent usually began with an e-mail sent the night before. Not only was Cameron working on the new machine learning tech, but he was integrating it into the project's back end. Working solo, without tickets, sprints, or a solid product specification, his output was unpredictable. Some mornings the developers could sit down and begin work straight away. Other mornings they first had to follow multi-point instructions from Cameron's e-mail to align their development environment with whatever changes had been made. Sometimes that just involved pulling down the latest code, sometimes it involved patching the database with queries he had attached to the e-mail, or running time-consuming commands to restructure or reindex the test data.

It was the *not knowing* that made it simultaneously interesting and exhausting. To say nothing of the sinking feeling that every additional day he spent on the back end was realistically moving the delivery date back by two days.

The code had also become significantly more complex than any of the developers were used to—by at least a whole order of magnitude. And the complexity was increasing with each passing day.

Features that had initially been presented as novel and exciting had become unwieldy additions to the codebase. Integration Hell loomed over the increasingly exasperated team. They joked: *Can't we just sack off this feature?* Then, with enough repetition, it stopping being a joke.

In time, the new joke became: *What if we just built an asynchronous API and put a person behind it?*

It was a frustrating process. Of that, everyone was in agreement. But they had also been working diligently. Soon enough, Evelyn and Robert's work was nearing completion. They had built out the dashboard to Cameron's specifications. It had a variety of tables, graphs, and other widgets—loaded with nonsense data, of course, but aesthetically pleasing all the same.

Robert sighed when he committed his last line of code to the project. He sighed in relief, he sighed in frustration, and he sighed in disappointment. He had just finished building the front end of a tool that would be used for purposes he fundamentally did not agree with.

Evelyn's professional dissatisfaction was less clear-cut. She could not put her finger on what exactly it was. Maybe it was the unwelcome stress of the daily integrations. Or maybe it was the feeling of unease from witnessing Cameron—to whom any problem was usually water off a duck's back—begin to crack under the pressure of the project.

Whatever the cause of their complaint, they were both burned out.

CHAPTER 7
A CLASSIC LIVE DEMO

THE CAMELCAT MARKETING office was rather typical of its industry. It was located in a small refurbished factory, complete with century-old exposed brick, I-beams, and paint. And it was just far enough from the city centre to both have the right post code and make anyone who attempted the commute on foot feel at least a little bit cheated.

It was an office that Oscar had not visited in his many years of doing business with Dru and CamelCat Marketing. Normally, when they would meet to discuss projects, a trendy meeting room in a central co-working space was provided. The refreshments were usually quite good.

On this day, however, Oscar came to the office.

It was 9:15 a.m. on Friday, just as rush hour was beginning to die down, and Oscar lingered outside. He peered through the small window in the heavy fire door that blocked access to the office. Having ascertained that there were at least a couple of people close by, he knocked the door sharply three times.

Moments passed, and no one answered. He was about to knock again when he heard someone approach from behind.

'Hi... can I help?'

It was Dru. He couldn't recall speaking with her since giving her hell on the phone a few weeks prior. This would be interesting.

He turned around and flashed his best smile.

'Good morning!' he beamed, placing one hand on the side of her arm as he extended the other for a handshake.

She shook his hand quickly and excused herself to unlock the door. Turning to the keypad, she entered a four-digit code and pushed the door open, holding it for him to enter first.

'Just let me drop my bag,' she told him, 'and I'll be right with you.'

As she walked briskly across the room to deposit her handbag in the corner office, Oscar waltzed over to the nearest desk and began making small talk with what looked to be one of the support staff. He enjoyed talking to the minions whenever he visited vendors; he was a man of the people. He took great pride in letting them know how much he respected the grunt work they did; a common refrain being that, for what they did, whatever they were being paid simply wasn't enough.

Dru soon returned. She motioned for Oscar to walk with her towards the office she had just come from.

Funny, he thought. *Why the round trip?*

'So to what do we owe the pleasure of your visit?' she asked.

Oscar wasn't normally one to be lost for words, but her question took him by surprise.

I'm here to see a demo of Accelerate, you idiot, he thought.

Dru raised her eyebrows somewhat, in anticipation of his response.

They entered her office.

'I'm here to see a demo of Accelerate, of course,' he eventually replied. Then, after some thought, added, 'Didn't Cam tell you?'

Dru's reaction said it all: Cameron had *not* told her. But at least if she was unprepared he'd be sure to get an honest view of how the project was progressing.

She reached for her phone, presumably to call Cameron and find out what he had set her up for.

'No need to call Cam,' Oscar said, motioning for her to put down the phone. 'He just said to drop by and he'd show me the work in progress. Only a few weeks 'til launch now; I'm excited to see this thing in action. So get one of your resources to load it up and blow me away!'

'Yes… of course.'

Dru led Oscar back out, towards the development team. She made some brief introductions and set the scene.

Upon learning that a client was in their midsts, the atmosphere changed. Robert seemed to sit up straighter in his chair, and Evelyn plastered on a smile.

Oscar picked up on it. He was, after all, a man of the people. After Dru had introduced him, he spoke to put them at ease: 'Yep, I'm the one who moves the goalposts!'

A few chuckles, and the attention turned to Robert. Dru asked him to fire up the latest version of Project Accelerate for a walkthrough.

He tapped out some commands on his laptop and the screen sprang to life. Text scrolled at high speed in a small black window.

'It'll take a minute to start up,' he explained. 'I've only just pulled in Cam's changes from last night, so bear in mind what you're looking at is super unstable right now. It'll be better once it's in production.'

That old chestnut.

Oscar observed the rapidly scrolling text and joked, 'It's like the Matrix!'

When the text came to a halt, Robert opened a new tab in his web browser and tapped in some numbers. He hit *enter* and a login screen sporting Purple Budgie Finance's logo appeared before him.

'Now, bear in mind we don't have proper test data,' he warned, 'so it's going to look a little barren at the moment. But I should be able to do a basic clickthrough to show you the various features.'

He entered the username **test** and the password **password**. He hit *enter* once more and a loading animation took over the screen. After a few moments, a dashboard not dissimilar to one of Purple Budgie Finance's existing systems revealed itself.

He clicked around a few boilerplate screens before navigating to the part of the platform that seemingly integrated with Cameron's machine learning code.

This was the part that Oscar had come to see. After the pressure he had piled on them, it was time to see the fruits of his labour. Would it make his life easier, or would he have to rip Dru a new one and drop her and her band of merry misfits like a sack of rotten potatoes?

'So, like I said, I only have real basic test data at the moment,' Robert re-warned everyone. 'But let's see what happens.'

A list of customer names populated the screen. He selected the first entry—a Mr Fakington whose stated category was *Funeral Cover Redemption*—and scanned down the list to find others who belonged to the same cohort. He clicked a button and another loading animation took over the screen. After twenty or so seconds of waiting, an explosion of confetti revealed the product best suited to Mr Fakington and his cohort: life insurance.

Life insurance. Life. Fucking. Insurance. For *dead* people.

Were they having a laugh?

Oscar was furious. 'Is this a joke?' he bellowed. 'Your gadget's telling me we should sell life insurance to dead people? Did you forget the shit we got for sending mailshots to grieving widows? We got dragged over the coals on national TV! First your blunder with that Owliphant nonsense, now this!'

The atmosphere was tense. Many of the developers looked to each other for clues on whether to speak up or slink away. Most were frozen on the spot.

Eventually, Evelyn took action. She grabbed Robert's keyboard and turned to Oscar.

'I'm sure it's just some bad test data,' she said. 'Sorry about that. What if I show you the graphing feature we've been working on? It breaks down the lifetime events of the cohort and shows you what the group is doing. *Single pane of glass* kind of thing.'

Oscar was ready to storm off. He had only been there a few minutes and already his time had been wasted. But curiosity got the better of him; what could this person possibly show him that would save the day?

Evelyn navigated back to the list of customers and selected a different option. Once more, the loading animation took over. But this time the wait was significantly longer.

Ten seconds.

Twenty.

Thirty.

Oscar had taken to shaking his head in disapproval. Subtle enough to appear genuine, but theatrical enough to be noticeable. He opened his mouth to say something cutting when the screen changed. But it was not the *single pane of glass* he had been promised: it was a full-screen error, followed roughly one second later by a complete system failure.

'Whoa!' exclaimed Kyle, who had largely been hovering out of harm's way. 'Our professor told us about Blue Screens of Death. From the nineties!'

'Shit, it's segfaulted!' Robert exclaimed, tapping at the keyboard to no avail.

Oscar had seen enough. The whole thing was a mess. The application fundamentally did not do what it was supposed to, it was unstable, and Cameron hadn't even bothered to show up.

He turned to Dru, occupying more of her personal space than was comfortable for either of them, and warned: 'This project is a complete clusterfuck, Dru. Fix. Your. Shit.'

Not waiting for a response, he stormed off.

CHAPTER 8
PASSING THE BUCK

Several hours after the disastrous show and tell—and quite late in the afternoon—Cameron finally waltzed through the door.

He only managed a few steps before Dru caught sight of him. She shot up like a rocket and made a beeline for him, grabbing him by the arm and dragging him off to the kitchenette at the far side of the office.

'Why the hell didn't you tell me Oscar was coming for a demo?!' she demanded, in a hushed voice that somehow managed to retain every speck of her fury. 'And why did the damned thing not work when Rob showed him?!'

'Oh shoot,' Cameron said, clicking his fingers. 'I thought that was next week. Honestly, the days are just blurring into one. I don't know whether I'm coming or going.'

Dru did not look impressed.

'On which note, do you realise it's almost the end of the day? You've got to keep normal hours, Cameron. And if there's a problem with the project, you need to be honest and tell me about it, not hide away and work late.'

Now it was Cameron who did not look impressed.

'Hey!' he snapped. 'There's nothing wrong with my code. I don't know what Rob did to fuck it up, but it works fine for me. If he fluffed the demo that's on him, not me.'

Dru was speechless.

Unbeknownst to the pair, Evelyn was on a tea run and—hidden around the corner—had heard their whole exchange.

CHAPTER 9
DEAR DRU

EVELYN HADN'T STUCK around for the rest of Cameron and Dru's conversation. She knew he'd throw her under the bus, too; she didn't need to hear the words spoken out loud.

When she arrived back at the developers' bank of desks empty-handed and silent, there were some puzzled looks. It took her a moment to snap out of her daze, and a moment longer to remember that she had been on a tea run.

What had thrown her the most was how out of character Cameron's comments had been. He had a reputation for being a bit of a loose cannon, and everyone knew that his technical prowess was balanced by his penchant for not thinking things through. But of all the things he was known for, throwing others under the bus was not normally one of them. At least not that anyone had witnessed.

She began to wonder what previous failings she had been blamed for. Was *that* the reason she hadn't seen a pay rise in two years?

After a little coaxing from her colleagues, she blurted out what she had overheard. *Better to rip off the plaster,* she thought.

The reaction was mixed. Some of the developers were used to management blaming them for their failings, while others were horrified at the notion of such a thing happening beneath their nose. Robert was silent. Like Evelyn, he seemed to be dwelling on the implications of the situation. At least others were outraged on his behalf.

Soon enough, the conversation turned to toxic management in general, with some of the older members of the team trading war stories, taking turns to one-up each other.

As the stories flowed, Evelyn—who had not said a word since sharing the news of Cameron's treachery—began to draft a letter:

> Dear Drusilla,
>
> It is with regret that I must tender my resignation from the role of Senior Software Developer at CamelCat Marketing.
>
> As per the terms of my contract, I will work a notice period of one month starting from today.
>
> If there is anything you would like me to focus on during my remaining time with the company, please let me know.
>
> Regards,
>
> Evelyn

CHAPTER 10
HALF A PIANO

EVELYN AND CHARLIE went back years. They met as colleagues at an advertising agency, where Evelyn had been hired into her first real job, and Charlie had been tasked with mentoring her. Though they eventually went their separate ways—Evelyn to sling code at a couple more agencies before CamelCat Marketing, and Charlie to lead the development team at boutique agency Half A Piano—Charlie still played an active role in mentoring her friend.

They did not see each other as often as Charlie would like, but once every two or three months they would meet for coffee after work. Evelyn would invariably unload her current frustrations, and Charlie would duly listen to them, somehow managing to channel them into a nugget of practical, actionable career advice.

It was not clear if Evelyn realised she was still being mentored, but Charlie preferred it that way; by keeping things informal, she had managed to talk her friend out of a number of rash decisions over the years.

When Evelyn sent her the short message, *u free to chat?*, Charlie knew that something was up.

They met after work at a trendy wine bar, just a short walk from CamelCat Marketing's office. It occupied the space beneath a railway arch and comprised of a lengthy bar made from reclaimed wood, a line of bar stools, and patio furniture spread through the rest of the space. The whole bar took on the orange glow of the halogen heaters that kept the punters warm.

Evelyn and Charlie were sat at the bar.

'How are things at HAP?' Evelyn asked. 'Still expanding the team?'

Charlie could see where this was going: Evelyn had the itch again. Last time, it was her worry that she had plateaued working with the same old tech. What would it be this time?

Charlie cut straight to the chase, and asked, 'Are we bored at CamelCat, Ev?'

Evelyn pulled a face. It wasn't quite a smile or a grimace, but something in-between. It was simultaneously cheeky, apologetic, and not sorry at all.

'I kind of quit,' she admitted.

Charlie closer her eyes. A kind of ocular facepalm.

'Oh Evy, you quit?'

Evelyn nodded. 'One month, then I'm officially fucked.'

This wasn't what Charlie had prepared for. An itch for leadership, or the desire to work with more exciting tech? Sure. But nothing so drastic.

'What happened?' was all she could say, as her brain raced to assemble a brand new pep talk.

Evelyn turned away from Charlie to cross her arms and lean against the bar.

'I don't have many lines, but today one of them was crossed.' As Charlie listened intently, she continued: 'There was a fuck up at work. A big one. Probably lost a client. And I heard the CTO use Rob as a scapegoat.'

'Rob's your colleague?'

'Yeah, he works with me on the front-end stuff. And that's the really stupid bit—it wasn't even the front-end code that fucked up! Cam did such a lazy job of passing the buck. He won't let anyone help out, and when it all goes wrong he blames everyone but himself. And I'm sure he tried to blame me, too.'

Conspiracy Mode engaged. This had the potential to be an interesting conversation. But was the damage already done?

'Do you know that for certain?' Charlie asked.

Evelyn shook her head. 'No, but does it matter? If he'll do it to Rob, he'll do it to me. He didn't know I could hear him; I was round the corner.'

Charlie considered the situation at some length before responding. How would *she* have felt in that situation? Without more context, it was hard to tell. But Evelyn wasn't here to examine the minutiae of the situation; she was here to get something off her chest. And, Charlie feared, to ask a favour.

'That's rough, Ev,' Charlie eventually said, consoling her with a light touch on the shoulder. 'And in your situation, I might even have done the same. I do wish you'd come chat with me *before* giving your notice, though.'

A visible panic spread across Evelyn's face.

'So you're not hiring?' she asked.

Charlie smiled.

'We are. But, honestly, I can't promise you anything. You'd have to interview with someone else, and if you joined the team, our relationship would have to change. So I want you to think carefully about this. Is HAP somewhere you really want to be, or is it just a solution to your current situation?'

'Oh, no, I definitely want it,' Evelyn said enthusiastically.

But Charlie cut her off: 'Sleep on it, Ev. Send me your CV and I'll pass it along, but sleep on it first. Then when you wake up, ask yourself the question again. Make sure it's right for you. And if it's not, I'll help you find something else.'

It was advice steeped in equal parts concern and selfishness. When a former colleague threatened to become a future colleague, the stakes were high—the intervening friendship would always be difficult to navigate.

Charlie finished her drink, and caught the attention of the bartender to request another round.

As Evelyn took her drink, a sheepish look crossed her face. Evidently, there was more.

Charlie narrowed her eyes. 'What else have you done?'

'Nothing bad!' Evelyn protested. 'I just invited Rob to join us. I kind of want him to apply to your place too...'

CHAPTER 11
THE FALLOUT

WHEN MONDAY MORNING ROLLED AROUND, Dru was conspicuous by her absence. Cameron was also absent, but that was less strange.

Would people notice? she wondered. Perhaps not.

The weekend had not been a fun one. Evelyn's resignation had thrown a spanner in the works, for sure. How exactly it would affect the team's velocity, Dru was not certain—she really needed to get more involved in that side of things—but the effect on morale would be huge. Evelyn was well-liked by everyone.

But the double whammy came when Robert, at 11:50 p.m. the night before, e-mailed a resignation letter of his own. If the departure of fun-loving and wacky Evelyn would be a blow to the team, the simultaneous departure of calm and predictable Robert would surely make everyone wonder: what the hell was going on?

Robert had been more direct in his letter of resignation than Evelyn. He spoke about his general dissatisfaction with the recent direction of the company, and his inability to get through to Cameron. The matter of Cameron's betrayal *was* addressed, but only as a minor point among other frustrations.

Dru knew a little bit about Robert's situation: he was a high earner, lived modestly, and had savings. The same was true of his spouse. He also cared deeply about the impact of his work on the world. All of this taken together made him a flight risk whenever times were bad.

Dru didn't like to think that way. But she could not ignore that Robert had the luxury to pick and choose his work. Even so, it still came as a shock.

Eventually making her appearance in the office, Dru looked around and surveyed her staff. They really were a great bunch of people. And now she had to break the news that their already-struggling team was soon to get smaller. And in such a tough market, no less! Would she even be able to hire decent replacements?

She walked over to Robert, tapped him on the shoulder, leant over, and asked quietly to speak with him in her office.

Once seated, she cut to the chase: 'So, obviously you know what we're about to talk about. I got your e-mail last night.' She waited to see if he would offer an initial comment. When he did not, she continued: 'I'll be honest, Rob, I was really surprised. I didn't see this coming. But the more I read your e-mail, the more I think I understand. I remember when I first interviewed you, how passionately you spoke about the company aligning with your personal values. And I guess we haven't lived up to that standard lately.'

'No,' Robert shook his head. 'We haven't. And honestly, I'm gutted about that. It's like this great thing has been slipping away, right in front of my eyes.'

'I want to talk a little bit about that in a moment,' Dru responded, 'but first I think I need to address a pretty serious issue. Obviously Cameron said something on Friday that I guess was the straw that broke the camel's back. I'm sorry you heard that. Your ability and work ethic has never been in question. And it wasn't right that he got frustrated and tried to blame you for what happened during the demo. I'm not a techie, but even I know live demos are just asking for trouble.'

She looked for a smile. Anything to suggest her joke had landed well, and reinforced the message. If she was going to lose him, she at least wanted him to know that there was no ill will on her side.

But Robert was a tough one to read. He may have chuckled on the inside, he may not have. He may have gained a tiny bit of appreciation for her empathy, or he may have been disgusted that she had attempted a joke during such a conversation.

'On the subject of the work we've been doing, though...' she swiftly moved on. 'I just have to be honest with you again Rob. I want more than anything for this company to do pure ethical marketing. It's the reason I get out of bed in the morning. Literally. But it's a small niche. Maybe one day it'll take over the industry, but it's not easy to source the kind of projects we want to work on. Sometimes it happens, and those are the days I can't stop smiling, but the rest of the time we just need to pick the least-offensive projects available to keep the lights on. I know it's not ideal.'

Robert nodded. 'I guess the problem is that we've been taking on a lot more projects like that recently.'

'We have,' Dru agreed.

The implication was fairly obvious, but she didn't want to spell it out: the business was struggling to get by with its preferred model.

Robert drew in a deep breath. 'In that case, I think I've definitely made the right choice. I only get one life, and I need to be doing good with it. If that's no longer possible here, then I've got to find somewhere else.'

Dru nodded lightly. That was that. What Robert wanted, CamelCat Marketing could no longer provide. She could hardly begrudge him sticking to his principles—she had known what they were from Day One. If anything, she felt disappointed with herself for failing to be a better business owner and leader.

It was times like these that she could really use her business partner for emotional support, but she had given Cameron an earful after receiving Robert's e-mail. She called him shortly after midnight and really let him have it, hanging up before he could even defend himself. Ironic, in some ways. Not her finest hour.

She finished up her conversation with Robert as well as she could manage, and saw him out the door before sending a message to Evelyn, asking for a quick chat. In the thirty seconds between hitting *Send* and Evelyn making moves toward her, Dru sat with her head flat against her desk. It was *not* a smiley day.

The conversation with Evelyn was considerably shorter. After the usual pleasantries, Evelyn got straight to the point: her old mentor had offered her a job and it would be a great career move —no hard feelings, nothing that could be done.

For the briefest of moments, Dru wondered whether Robert and Evelyn were in on it together, just having a laugh. But it was not a joke, and from what she could tell, Evelyn was probably interviewing well before the fateful events of last Friday. It was just bad timing, and a sign that her finger was not as firmly on the team's pulse as she thought.

Oh well, she thought. *Two awkward conversations down, one huge one to go.*

CHAPTER 12
SOME HARSH TRUTHS

THE NEXT AWKWARD conversation was with the whole team. The company's future was in danger, and they deserved to know where they stood.

Dru stood before the assembled team, preparing to tell them about the harsh reality they now faced.

'I have some news to share,' she began. 'First of all, Cameron's going to be taking some personal time away from the business for the next few weeks. Also—and it's come as bit of a surprise, but we wish them well—next month Rob and Ev will be leaving us.'

Some murmuring erupted amongst the team. It was to be expected, but was not the start Dru wanted to get off to. She had more troubling news to deliver, after all.

She noticed Robert and Evelyn turning to look at each other. Evelyn seemed rather shocked by the news, whereas Robert did not. He really was full of surprises.

Dru gave the team a moment to digest the news, then called for quiet. The murmuring trailed off.

'I also want to let everyone know about some recent developments here at CamelCat Marketing. As you all know, Purple Budgie are our largest client. We've been doing work for them for the last five years, and I'm not sure if everyone knows the ins and outs, but they account for a sizeable chunk of our revenue.'

Dru paused, unsure what exactly she was going to say next. The words eventually came, though she was not sure from where.

'Unfortunately, they're in the process of reassessing their vendors, and we're on a shortlist of companies they may cease partnering with.'

Not entirely a lie, but far enough from the truth to make the message more palatable. Better than admitting that they were being punished for working on ads that everyone in the company—herself included—had advised against.

'If we lose PB, then honestly? We're in trouble.' Her next sentence had to come quickly, as the murmuring was picking back up with a vengeance. 'But everyone, listen… Accelerate is our chance to stop that from happening. If we can wow them with this project, we're safe. I know this is a lot to take onboard, and I'm so sorry to dump this on you all, but if we stand any chance of getting this right, we have to know what's at stake. As a team, we can come through this!'

The *motivational* part of the speech came too late. Or was not convincing enough. Or had simply not been heard over the multitude of conversations that had broken out amongst the staff.

'How are we going to finish Accelerate without Cam?' James asked directly. 'And I wish you both luck and all, but do we stand any chance if Ev and Rob are leaving?'

The fact was that Evelyn and Robert *would* be around long enough to see the end of the project. But Dru did not get the chance to share that fact before the next question came her way.

'Forget that,' said Sam, one of the sales representatives. 'If Accelerate is our lifeline, we need to be out selling this piece of crap now. Not just to PB, but to anyone who will have it. I'm not sitting on my hands for a month just to lose my job because we missed a deadline.'

That set everyone off. Up until that point, some of the team hadn't connected the dots and registered the potential severity of the situation. Now, everyone had. Within moments, phones came out and frantic tapping ensued. Were they messaging partners, or recruiters? Had Dru just made the biggest mistake of her career?

The questions continued to come in thick and fast, each one leaving Dru even less time to respond than the one before.

'How much money do we have left?' Kyle asked, immediately adding, 'How will you choose who goes if we lose PB? I don't think it should be any of the developers.'

That comment set *everyone* off. A mini culture war erupted between the various departments, and Dru lost complete control of the room. She slunk back off to her office as they tore into each other, sinking into her chair and burying her face in her hands.

She was startled out of her stupor when a sharp knock came at the glass door. Alice stood on the other side.

CHAPTER 13
A HIDDEN SKILL

DRU'S GLASS office had a different feel from the wider open-plan office it sat within. Excepting the mess of cables behind desks and the various conference swag atop them, the open-plan office was neat and tidy. It was clean and minimalist. It was modern, after all. Dru's private corner, by contrast, was anything but. Team photos clung to the glass walls with Blu Tack, old computer equipment littered the floor, and the door was blocked from fully opening by stacked boxes of branded CamelCat Marketing apparel.

Alice looked around. She was seldom in Dru's office; it took a few moments to adjust.

'What would you like to talk about?' Dru asked. 'If it's about job security—'

Alice cut her off with a shake of the head. She took a moment to consider the exasperated look on Dru's face. Did she know how badly she had just messed up? She must, surely?

'I'm not worried,' Alice answered.

Dru scoffed. The reply, *You should be,* hung in the air, even if the words never came.

Alice sat down and shuffled her chair forward. She explained: 'Look, Dru, you're not stupid. It's obvious you know how that just went. I mean, look outside…' She motioned behind her. 'It's full on *Animal Farm* out there right now. Everyone's spooked, and that group of humans are doing what humans do best: freaking the fuck out.'

'I know, I know!' Dru cried. 'I just wanted to be honest with you all. Isn't that supposed to be one of our values? We even tell people the bad stuff when they interview with us. It usually works out well.'

It was true; Dru conducted all final interviews at CamelCat Marketing, and she made a point of telling people *exactly* what they would be letting themselves in for.

Alice recalled *her* interview. She was told in no uncertain terms that the tech was out of date, and it would frustrate her to no end. But she was also told that she would have the opportunity to help modernise. The honesty was refreshing.

'This is different, though,' Alice explained. 'This wasn't

giving people a balanced view of things. This was all problems and no solutions. You know everyone's working as hard as they can; no motivational speech is going to magically increase capacity. Everyone knows that. Then you mention Cameron being off. And everyone knows what he did, so they probably all think he's either quit or been kicked out.' She took a moment, then continued with a softer tone: 'I get we're in trouble, but it was just problem, problem, problem, without any solutions. People look up to you, Dru; even if your solutions are crap, you still have to bring them.'

It took a while for Dru to say anything. It was understandable; Alice was not normally one to rock the boat, and that dose of truth was as blunt as the one Dru had just delivered to the team.

'I guess that makes sense...' was all she could muster.

Alice smiled in a kind, apologetic manner.

'Look, it's not my place to tell you how to run your company, but I've seen enough projects fail that I can tell Accelerate's circling the drain. If it's honestly our only chance to save CamelCat, we can't continue with business as usual—if you think Friday was a disaster, just wait until launch day. We have to do something radical with the tech.'

'What, you want Cam's job?' Dru enquired.

Alice couldn't help but laugh out loud. She absolutely did *not* want Cameron's job. She had gotten a taste of that in a previous role, and the stress was not her bag. Maybe in another company it would be different, but she had no desire to find out.

'No thank you,' she answered. 'But over the years I've learned a thing or two that I think could help us. If I'm being presumptuous, I apologise, but I'm happy to jump in the driving seat to help us course correct, if you want.'

'What would you do?' Dru asked, after a moment of silent contemplation.

Alice reached for the phone in the middle of the desk.

'How would you feel if I spoke to Oscar at PB?'

'I suppose that would be okay?' Dru answered. She began dialling the number for Purple Budgie Finance, pausing on the final digit to ask, 'Just... what about?'

'I could be wrong, but I have a feeling we've got the wrong end of the stick about what they actually need. I want to ask him and find out.'

It was a gutsy move, but needs must. Alice's colleagues were at the point of implosion, and she desperately needed a light at the end of the tunnel to get them all back on track. They had just been told that finishing Project Accelerate was the path back to stability and glory, and she intended to clear that path for them.

Dru punched in the final number, and after a long wait Oscar answered.

'Hello?'

'Hi, Oscar?'

'Yes?'

'Hi, it's Alice here; one of the developers from CamelCat. I'm just here with Dru. I hoped I could get five minutes of your time, just to ask a few questions about Accelerate?'

There was a brief silence.

Finally, Oscar answered: 'Okay, I suppose. What kind of questions? Do we need to get Cameron on, too?'

Alice replied quickly, to preempt any questions about Cameron: 'No, it's okay. Cam's actually off today. I'm just picking up in his absence. As we're getting really close now with Accelerate, I just wanted to make sure there weren't any edge cases or important bits we've missed. Is that okay?'

Again, there was a brief silence. When Oscar spoke, he sounded impatient. Like a busy parent on a school run who had stood still just long enough to be collared by a roaming missionary.

'Sure, fine. What do you want to know?'

'That great!' Alice replied. 'I'll try not to take up too much of your time. But, just to go back to basics, could you sum up in a few words the one thing Accelerate will help you achieve over there at Purple Budgie Finance?'

'More sales, obviously!' Oscar barked.

There was frustration in his voice. The missionary's very first question might have been one too many, and the appetite to play along was ebbing. Alice knew she would have to get to the point, and quickly.

'Of course,' she replied. 'And that's a given, obviously. We're hard at work making sure that happens for you. I just wanted to probe a bit deeper and understand what specifically is missing from your current toolset that stops that from happening? You know; make sure we're filling all the gaps.'

'It's the ML,' he said. 'Only ML can do the same thing a person can do.'

The frustration was still present, but it seemed safe enough to probe a little deeper. So Alice continued: 'Makes sense. So it's basically a scaling issue? At the moment you have people doing this work, but there's too much of it?'

'Yeah, pretty much. It used to be a one-man job, but *somehow* we've managed to do a lot of business this year, and there's just not enough hours in the day.'

'Interesting…' Had she a beard, Alice would have been stroking it in contemplation. She continued to probe: 'And how have your people been doing this work until now?'

'In a spreadsheet,' Oscar answered, matter-of-factly.

Fucking spreadsheets. Why was it that the root of all software projects was someone's runaway spreadsheet?

'Interesting…' Alice said again. There was less conviction this time, but she needed a segue into her next question: 'So you mentioned there weren't enough hours in the day—is that just a numbers thing? Could the spreadsheet have handled the problem if you had more people available to use it? Or does it just stop working at a certain point? I want to preempt any scaling issues before we get into proper testing with you.'

That last bit was a lie, but essential to hide the true nature of the conversation. Alice was digging deep to find the underlying problem that Accelerate was intended to solve. Her intention was to figure out what an MVP could look like, and by probing about the underlying problem she could avoid a messy spiral into solutionising.

'No, it's just how much manpower we have to throw at the thing. It doesn't crash or anything like that. But you need people to input the sales data, and you need people to look for the patterns. The effort increases with each new customer.'

'And where did this process originate?' Alice enquired.

'Ah, now that was my idea!' Oscar, for the first time in the conversation, was animated. 'Ages ago, when we had less customers, you could just eyeball it. Used to be Paul's job, then he left and it fell to me. But once we got more customers, the only way to get a good view was to dump it all into a spreadsheet. Because you can't really sort or filter it in the CRM. So once it's in there, you can order it a certain way, and *then* eyeball it. It was my crowning achievement, until it got too time-consuming to keep up with. Hence Accelerate.'

The CRM was a factor Alice had not expected. But she sensed an opportunity.

'Your CRM; that's the one we built for you, right?'

'Correct.'

'Excellent. And one final question, if that's okay?' Alice gave Oscar a moment to object, which he did not. 'Other than filtering and ordering, is there anything else that you do in the spreadsheet that you can't do in the CRM?'

'I guess the SKUs? They're in the list, but you can't search by them. And trying to group them in your head is next to impossible because they're just numbers that don't really mean anything.'

'Interesting.' Alice paused to mentally summarise everything she had just learned, and to give Dru a thumbs up. 'That's all really helpful Oscar, thank you. I'm confident what we're building will solve this problem for you.'

CHAPTER 14
A DIFFERENT APPROACH

WHILE OSCAR EXPLAINED Purple Budgie Finance's spreadsheet woes, Alice had been jotting down anything that sounded important on a pad of sticky notes. By the time the conversation had ended, several notes were laid out haphazardly before her.

Dru had been silent throughout the exchange. She listened in and watched as Alice scribbled out her notes, nodding her head where it made sense, and peering at what Alice was writing where it did not.

After spending a few moments tidying up the notes so they all faced the same direction, Alice leaned back. She held her hand to her face and tapped against her lip, seeming to take stock of what she had written.

Dru looked to her in anticipation. There was a big revelation coming, but what was it?

Finally, Alice spoke.

'So… this is an overview of *why* Project Accelerate exists.' She gestured at the notes, then thought some more before continuing: 'Oscar said some interesting things, the main one being that we're essentially just replacing a spreadsheet. A spreadsheet that only exists because our CRM is missing a few basic features.'

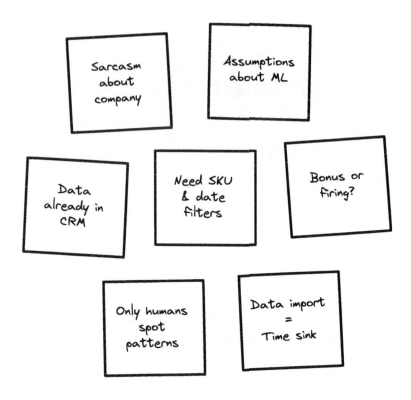

'And the *machine learning* bit,' Dru chimed in. 'That was important too.'

Alice pursed her lips. 'I didn't really hear anything that warranted ML, if I'm being honest,' she answered. 'I mean, sure, a human looks over the data to make a decision, but it's pretty basic stuff: if they bought X, we offer them Y. It gets a *little* bit more complicated than that, but not much. And it's not like we have enough data to make proper use of ML anyway; a generalised off-the-shelf solution is the best we could hope for.'

'That's what ML-Cast was, right?' Dru asked.

'Correct.' Alice turned her attention back to the notes,

tapping on the one in the middle. 'This,' she said, 'is what we should be building. If we added some advanced filters and sorting to their CRM, we could eliminate 80% of what they currently do in that spreadsheet. And this...' she pointed to the note at the bottom-right, 'this wouldn't even be a thing, because the data would already be in the right place.'

'I see.'

Dru was following the logic, but was still a little confused. What Alice was saying made sense, but then so had Cameron's plan to bring machine learning to CamelCat Marketing. Was Alice a genius or a fool?

She would find out.

'What about that last 20%, then?' she asked.

Alice deflected the question: 'Let's come back to that. Because I think there's another force at work pushing this *machine learning* agenda, and it all centres around these two points.'

She removed all but two of the sticky notes.

'This,' Alice continued, 'is what's at stake for Oscar. There was a moment where he was sarcastic about PB's success. It was ever so brief, but it was clear as day: there stood a man who had stopped believing in the vision. He blamed us for those awful ads, right?'

Shit. Had that become common knowledge?

'Well...' was all Dru could muster.

'It's neither here nor there,' Alice said. 'Fact is, shit rolls downhill, so if *we* got it in the neck from him, then *he* got it in the neck from someone else. And Oscar seems like the kind of person who usually gets his way, so I'd put money on him reacting poorly to that kind of telling off. He's got one foot out the door, for sure. Except...'

Except?

'What if he pulls off the impossible?' Alice asked. 'A veritable *Hail Mary*? Commission a project to automate a process the company was about to give up on, using mysterious tech that no one understands? It's a roll of the dice that will either hasten his exit or secure his position for the foreseeable future.'

It wasn't the most outlandish thing Dru had heard recently, but was tweaking the old CRM really the way to go? The developers thought she didn't understand tech, but over the years she'd picked up enough to make sense of their veiled comments, and the consensus was clear: the CRM was a piece of crap; something that should have been sent to live on a farm upstate years ago.

'But if he's expecting mysterious tech, would he even be happy with some tweaks to the CRM?' Dru asked. 'And would the devs, for that matter?'

Alice chuckled. 'Yeah, if you think you have a mutiny on your hands now, just wait 'til we tell them they have to work on the CRM again! People will grumble, for sure, but it's a light at the end of the tunnel, and at the end of the day I think they'll be happy about that. All that old, crappy tech that sits underneath it we can fix another day. And if I'm right, all Oscar wants is a big win. ML might *sound* impressive, but people will be more impressed if we can make this slot right into their existing workflows. No new creds, no expensive training, just value from Day One. And if they're not e-mailing CSVs full of customer info around, they'll not fall foul of any data laws.'

'God, I hadn't even thought of that!' Dru said.

Alice smiled, then pulled a thoughtful face.

'You know, I think I know someone who's between contracts at the moment. A good, solid backender who could help us get this over the line. I'll give him a call.'

'And he could do what you're proposing?' Dru asked. 'Get these recommendations coming through in the old CRM?'

'I think he could,' Alice answered. 'In fact, the more I think about this, the simpler it gets. They only add new products every quarter, right?'

Dru nodded her head. 'Yes, I believe so.'

'Great. So the logic changes seldom enough that we could just put one dev on it for a few hours every quarter to add the new products into the config. And because they only run this report once a day, the data doesn't even need to be fresh; we could churn through it all on a batch job at midnight. Then it really does just become as simple as letting them filter through it.'

Dru was suddenly excited. She had been sceptical, but now it was starting to become clear. Oscar's ask was almost entirely focused around playing with the data they already had. The *recommendation* piece—though superficially the most important aspect—was almost secondary to the real problems he and his colleagues faced. She didn't share Alice's confidence in ripping out the machine learning component, but maybe this was one of those *machine learning is just IF statements* things the developers joked about?

She wanted to be sure.

'Just walk me through how you're proposing we do this without ML,' she asked. 'This is a big thing for me to sign off on. How do we do that final 20% you mentioned?'

Alice smiled and began to explain: 'It's really quite simple. All they need is to recommend a product based on what else the customer has recently bought or interacted with. That's dead simple; you could map that out right now if I gave you the data and a whiteboard. And as it happens, we *do* have that data. How all the products relate to each other; it's what we were training ML-Cast with. Now, it's a boring job that someone's going to really hate us for, but we can manually map all of those products together in a config file, then just get the CRM to look them up. If there are multiple recommendations, we can give some weighting based on other criteria, but it doesn't get much more complicated than that.'

'And if the logic isn't right?' Dru enquired.

Alice's eyes widened. 'We could have it ping back to us!' she declared excitedly. 'We could have a little slider or feedback button or something. One of those *more like this* and *less like this* things. If the system makes a bad recommendation, they can click to tell us, we get a report, and as far as they're concerned it's an intelligent system that's constantly learning.'

Was that dishonest or genius? Dru couldn't quite decide. But it made sense.

In a moment of clarity, she made a decision: she would bet the company on Alice's proposal. They weren't likely to succeed anyway, so why not go out trying something radical?

CHAPTER 15
RALLYING THE TROOPS

THE GRUMBLES, chatter, and speculation had not stopped. If anything, it had taken on a whole new life since Alice disappeared into Dru's office, and intensified when she returned and called an all-hands meeting.

Had the cruel hands of capitalism already claimed their first victim? Was Alice the first to go, in some attempt to buy a few more days of runway for the company? Had Alice volunteered her job to protect those of her colleagues? The suspense was overwhelming.

No work had been done since Dru's clumsy announcement. Many had taken to openly updating their CVs, while some had begun to reach out to recruiters and old bosses. It never hurt to be prepared. And then Stephen—a sales intern three months into his year in industry—had left for a cigarette break and not come back.

The conversation abated when Dru called their attention and Alice spoke. She didn't begin with words like 'unfortunately', 'as you all know', or 'it's been a pleasure'. Instead, she began with a business-as-usual, matter-of-fact, 'So...'

Not what they were expecting.

'So...' she said. 'We've got a short amount of time to deliver Accelerate. I've discussed some ideas with Dru, and I have a pretty good idea how we can do it.'

She pulled over a nearby flipchart, found a blank sheet of paper, and drew a box with the word *Accelerate* inside it. Her back turned to the assembled team, she stared at it for several moments, before grabbing the edge of the sheet and tearing it away, ripping the drawing in half. She balled up the paper and tossed it clear over everyone's heads.

'That's what we need to do to Accelerate,' she said.

A dramatic opening, but somewhat confusing. Were they going to toss it over to some other team? Or bury their heads in the sand until the problem simply went away?

'Uh...' someone began, but Alice cut them off with a chuckle.

'Forgive the melodrama. I reckon we can throw a lot of the project away. There's stuff we've built that's cool—don't get me wrong—but isn't strictly required to make the client happy. There's a model we used at the last place I worked, to figure this stuff out...'

She tugged off the rest of the sheet to expose a fresh piece of paper. On it she drew two lines, creating a grid. She labelled the axes: *Users asked for it* on the X axis, and *Users are using it* on the Y axis.

She stood back and observed the grid. Several people craned their necks to get a clear look. Fortunately, it was easy to read, even from a slight distance. She was one of those annoying people whose handwriting was neat and uniform. Which was bizarre in her line of work, really. No one wrote with a pen and paper anymore.

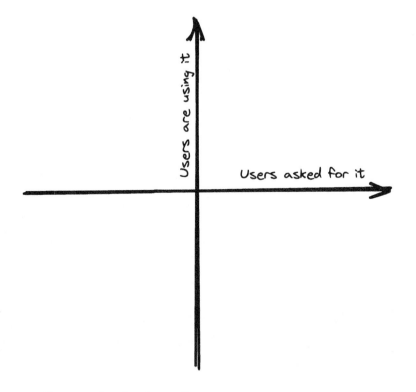

She turned to face her colleagues.

'What if I said you could map any feature on this grid? And what if I said that, by figuring out where a feature lives on this grid, we can decide how much effort—if any—to spend on it?'

'Give us an example?' James asked.

'With pleasure.' Alice wrote the words *Machine Learning* on a sticky note and placed it off to the side of the grid. 'Where do you think this would go?'

A few hands tentatively went up. It was interesting, but was a corporate whiteboarding session *really* what the team needed right now?

Alice picked on James.

'I guess it's in the top-right?' he speculated.

Alice nodded. 'That makes sense, doesn't it? It's the one feature that sits at the heart of Accelerate, so of course it's something the client has asked for, and they're going to use it. But let's take a step back and think about it for a moment. Did they *actually* ask for it?'

'It was in the spec,' Evelyn interjected.

'It was,' Alice replied, 'but that's just a suggestion of how to solve their problem—*use machine learning*. What did they *actually* ask us to build for them?'

There was silence. No one was in the mood for mind games or being made to feel stupid. So they offered no suggestions.

After a few moments, Alice provided the answer: 'They wanted a way to solve a problem they were facing. A problem that involved copying data into a spreadsheet, manipulating it a bit, and then making a judgement. We may have been told, "Use machine learning to recommend new products to existing customers," but that's just one possible way to solve the problem. I just spoke to Oscar at PB and dug down into what problem Accelerate is intended to solve, and there's really no solid reason to use machine learning. Despite how it may *appear*, it's not actually what they asked for. Our remit is to solve problems, and ML is one possible solution, but it's also something that, to be blunt, is not something we can pull off. We don't have the skills, and our dataset is *tiny*. So when we think about where to put this sticky note, I reckon it's one of the bottom two corners. You can argue that maybe someone asked for it, but I guarantee they won't be using it... our tests are showing that it's not reliable—even the tests that go well are giving bad results half the time; we'd be better off flipping a coin! The fact is, we have way too little data to make machine learning work, and even if that weren't the case, I'm not convinced that a basic decision tree can't do a better job.'

She stuck the note in the bottom-left corner of the grid and wrote the words *Waste of Time* in large letters. She then proceeded to label the other three quadrants of the grid.

Now this was interesting. Could they just label problematic features a *Waste of Time* and sack them off? That would be a game changer. But they feared not.

James decided to ask.

'So it *looks* like ML is a Mission Critical feature, but it's actually a Waste of Time? I guess that makes sense. But what's with the others? Is there more stuff we can reclassify to cut some scope?'

'Quite possibly!' Alice answered, visibly happy that someone was engaging. 'It's about looking at each thing we're building and asking really hard questions about why we're building it, and whether it will be useful to the user. So the Mission Critical stuff is probably fairly obvious: it's all the *no-brainer* stuff… you ask for a car, so we need to include wheels. Then in the top-left there's ideas that may be a Stroke of Genius; features that no one has asked for, but we've built anyway and they turn out to solve a problem and be extremely useful. It's great when it works out, but it's also quite risky, and when you're against the clock like we are, probably not worth attempting. This is a limited-scope project, after all, not a skunkworks.'

That made sense. And several features came to mind that had sucked up valuable development time, and had excited everyone, but no one had actually asked for. Like the advanced analytics features, which were essentially icing on the cake to distract from the fact that the cake wasn't properly cooked.

Alice continued: 'The Waste of Time label I feel is self-explanatory. That's where I reckon ML probably sits. Just anything we've built that misses the mark entirely. Like if you gave a car square wheels. Then finally, there's situations where Vision and Reality Are Not Equal. This is where you've made a decision based on an assumption about the future, or you misunderstood what the problem was, or you understood the problem but you misunderstood what a suitable solution might be. And this is where we might also find a lot of our features, because we're building for another company at a distance, and aren't down in the weeds with them.'

That also made sense. And offered hope that some more of the project could be descoped.

But they couldn't just throw stuff out, could they?

Robert now decided to speak up, and ask that very question: 'So just to be clear, you're saying we go through the project, feature by feature, and decide what to throw out and what to double down on? No matter how much time we've already sunk into it?'

Alice nodded her head. 'That's exactly what I'm suggesting. It's still going to be tight, but I think swapping out the ML for a decision tree saves us a lot of time whilst also getting the accuracy up, and if we port what we've done into their existing

CRM we make it an easier system to use and don't have to build all that admin functionality that I know we haven't got round to yet. And that's just scratching the surface based on one phone call I had with PB. I bet if we spent the rest of the day doing a deep dive on this, we'll be able to cut weeks of dev time. *And still deliver something that solves their core problem.*'

As much as everyone was still reeling from Dru's earlier faux pas, it was an enticing prospect. To be quick and agile again. To throw away bad code and burn shit down! And to have a light at the end of the tunnel. Some would still seek new opportunities— they had families to support, after all—but the impending collapse of the company no longer felt quite so certain. Maybe it would even survive?

CHAPTER 16
THE NEW WORK IN PROGRESS

MICHAEL WAS A VETERAN SOFTWARE DEVELOPER. He had worked on all manner of systems, and had made all manner of mistakes. There wasn't a disaster known to IT that he hadn't witnessed first-hand. So to say that he had an acute awareness of how *not* to do things was an understatement.

Michael also owed Alice a favour, and was intrigued by the proposal she presented to him: help on a project that had as good as failed, that had caught the blowback of an all-too-typical AI scandal, and that held the fate of an entire company in its frail hands.

It was a proposal he accepted, out of morbid curiosity if nothing else.

With Cameron out of the office, it would fall to Michael to take over the back end, port whatever needed saving to Purple Budgie Finance's old CRM tool, and race against the clock to tweak existing features and build new ones in accordance with the team's new-found consensus on solving the spreadsheet problem.

It was a slow start, but after a few days of diving into the code and asking really stupid questions, Michael felt ready to begin. He started work first on the decision tree, making use of mock data while Dru and the juniors took on the thankless task of sanitising the real data.

After a week and a half of non-stop coding, he asked to arrange a new demo with Oscar. This caused some concern in his new colleagues. But the deadline was not going to move, and he felt they were getting close to having a quick and dirty MVP ready to show. It wouldn't be polished, and it may even look like a step backward from the last demo, but it would perform one task and perform it well. He wanted both Oscar and the team to see the power of that: of just doing one thing really well.

If time permitted (but *only* if time permitted), they would add one additional feature for the demo: a shower thought that had come from Julie. She had apparently been troubled by the *life insurance* debacle, and wondered what *she* would have liked to have happened had one of her relatives passed away. The idea she presented to the team was genius in its simplicity: a condolence note to the family and an easy, unobtrusive way to close down all of their deceased relative's accounts. She had posited that a condolence package could be added to the system and linked to funeral cover, with a human taking over to send the note whenever it popped up as a recommendation.

As a stretch goal, it was well-received. It would be easy to implement, would solve a very real problem, and would demonstrate to the client that past mistakes had been learned from. Some were even calling the simple idea a Stroke of Genius.

The decision to demo the product having been made, Oscar scheduled a visit for the following week, coinciding with the end of the team's active sprint. It was short notice, but was a deadline everyone could rally around.

CHAPTER 17
DEMO 2.0

WHEN OSCAR ARRIVED for the follow-up demo, he brought along his boss, Monica. The last demo being the shitshow that it was, the likelihood of this one being any better was slim. And if everything was going to go wrong, he wanted there to be no doubt exactly who had messed up.

Monica was greeted by Dru and introduced to a few members of the team. She shook the hand of Alice, who would be conducting the demo, and exchanged a pleasant smile with the remaining members of the development team who were gathered nearby.

While Alice set up the demo, Dru and Monica engaged in small talk about something mundane. Business trips, perhaps? Oscar wasn't really listening. He was keeping an eye on Alice. So far all she had done was log in to their CRM.

'So,' she said, gathering everyone's attention, 'this is the new system.'

Oscar did a double take. What on earth was going on? This wasn't the shiny new system they had been promised; it was the old system they'd already paid for!

Alice continued: 'You may notice that what I'm showing you here is your current CRM. We had originally designed a brand new interface for Accelerate, but after talking with Oscar we realised that your current manual process starts with an export from the CRM, and most of what you go on to do in a spreadsheet could actually be carried out inside the CRM too, if we just added a few features. This also has the added benefit of making it easier to train people up—they only have to learn the new features, not a whole new system.'

So *that* was the point of that odd phone call. But Oscar was still owed a shiny new system, and this didn't look like it.

Monica nodded approvingly.

'Show us how it works, then,' Oscar instructed.

Dru exchanged a glance with Alice, who took the mouse and navigated to a list of recent sales. She clicked a button to reveal a set of basic filters and narrowed the list to customers who had finalised a mortgage 11 months ago. A list of John and Jane Does appeared, with basic information about their mortgage deals in one column, and a checkbox in another.

Alice clicked a few of the checkboxes and a new button appeared: *Recommendations*. She clicked it, and a loading animation covered the screen.

They waited.

And waited.

This felt familiar. It was the same animation that had been the harbinger of failure in the first demo. Oscar knew it; for all their talk of being more efficient, this was the moment they would shit the bed.

Monica may not have picked up on it, but he could see the developers observing from a safe distance begin to fidget. He could feel the tension in the air. They had no confidence this thing would work.

But Alice was a good orator. While the others watched

nervously, she kept the mood light and distracted from the wait by quipping: 'We're working on a much nicer loading animation, of course. Should have all the nice visual tweaks done in a couple of days.'

Oscar could appreciate a good salesperson when he saw one.

Then, against all of his expectations, the loading animation disappeared and the table updated with a new column. In that new column was a product SKU and short descriptor for each recommendation.

'Would you like to have a look?' Alice asked.

Oscar nodded and sat in her chair. He scrolled through the list of recommendations, hunting for anything that was awry. Another insensitive recommendation, perhaps.

Monica watched over his shoulder.

He continued scrolling. Everything seemed to make sense. A year after taking out a mortgage they would normally prod the customer to shop around for a better building insurance policy, and there the recommendation was, front and centre.

In the mix was also a customer with a fixed-term mortgage of one year. That was sloppy test data; did one-year terms even exist? But the recommendation accompanying it—to consider remortgaging—was spot on.

'Now select a couple of them and hit the *Action* button,' Alice instructed.

Oscar did as he was told. A modal titled *Success* popped up with a generic message and animation.

'What's this?' he asked.

Dru offered an explanation: 'This is the best part. There's not much to show because this is just a test environment, but this effectively hooks into all your existing systems. You have e-mail templates in the CRM for most of your customer comms already, so this will select the right template and e-mail the customer for you. Or, if the action is something internal, it'll use the existing system to set a reminder, or e-mail the sales team to arrange a phone call with the customer, or whatever needs to happen.'

That was... unexpected. It was nothing they weren't already doing, of course, but it was now automated, end-to-end. It could actually save people a lot of time. Somehow, the recommendation algorithm felt like a footnote in the demo.

'On which note,' Alice said, gesturing to retrieve the mouse from Oscar, 'there's one more thing we've built in that we think you'll appreciate.'

She returned to the main screen and began the process anew, searching this time for customers who had recently cashed in a funeral cover policy.

'Last time we had a small hiccup in this area.'

Too bloody right. The reputational damage from that little 'hiccup' could have been huge. That was the kind of thing that got honest salespeople splashed across the front page of tabloids.

Alice generated recommendations for the customers, and again the room filled with tension. When eventually the loading animation disappeared, the recommendation presented was simple: *Internal: Condolence Package.*

'What's this?' Monica asked.

'In this scenario, we thought it could be nice to send some kind of condolence package to the customer's family,' Dru explained. 'Along with plain-English instructions on how to take over and wind down the account.'

'And again, this all uses your existing tech,' Alice elaborated. 'This could just send an e-mail to a suitable person on your team. Or depending what you want to send them, we could even hook into some third-party service to order a little package with a printed card.'

'I love it!' Monica exclaimed. 'And we could add more of these if we wanted?'

Alice nodded. 'Absolutely. Some things might require a little bit of dev work from us, but you'll probably be able to self-serve 90% of the time.'

Oscar had mixed feelings. He had prepared himself for a disaster, maybe even a fight. And why not? Prior to this, he had seen nothing to suggest that these clowns actually understood what they were supposed to be building, let alone *how* to build it. But this actually solved the problem, and automated a few other things along the way. If they delivered on time, Monica would be very happy indeed.

'Huh...' he muttered, 'you may just pull this off.'

CHAPTER 18
PREPARING TO LAUNCH

THE FINAL FEW days before launch felt like a sprint that would just not end. Not a *development* sprint, but a *sprint* sprint. The kind of sprint that leaves you doubled over, exhausted at the finish line.

The bulk of the tasks were complete, but there were fires burning and edge cases that did not quite work as expected. Nothing so bad that it would enrage Oscar, but a hundred small things, frustrating for the fact that, were there just a little bit more time, they would be easily squashed.

But, by and large, the client was happy. That was always a win.

Purple Budgie Finance had been treated to daily demos of the work in progress. Over a period of only a few short weeks they grew accustomed to experimenting, providing feedback, and seeing a fix as early as the following day. Even more novel was the inclusion in the process of those who would actually be using the tool. Through them, important nuances had been uncovered that neither Oscar nor the CamelCat Marketing developers had anticipated.

Each day, the developers would load a snapshot of recent production data and compare the CRM's recommendations against those produced by Oscar's manual process. Alice coded a script to report the discrepancies. It was a trivial task that had taken her almost no time at all, but it helped them learn where to make changes. Sometimes it was the model that was wrong, sometimes the data, and sometimes even the human who was carrying out the process manually!

It was fun and stressful in equal measure.

And if the pressure of rapidly iterating a solution to completion wasn't enough, Cameron's return to the office a week from Launch Day turned the dial up to 11.

People had got used to him not being around. They had become accustomed to others running meetings, to decisions being made by policy rather than whim... and Alice had grown accustomed to calling the shots, even if deep down she was looking forward to handing the reins back. Maybe not to Cameron, but to *someone*.

Initially, Cameron made some attempts to be useful. He offered to sit with Michael, to review his new code and check it was 'up to CCM standards'. But when he learned that Project Accelerate had been reimagined without a trace of machine learning, he coughed and spluttered his coffee. The silence that followed could only be described as mourning for his pet project, or possibly anger at the audacity of this stranger and his new approach.

No one knew that he had spent much of his time off assembling a presentation on his vision for the project, ready for the conference season.

After a couple of silent, inactive days, he began picking up some of the more interesting tasks that remained in the sprint. But he also began to silently revert commits that he disagreed with, causing problems when the other developers pulled down the latest code and found it to be suddenly broken.

Which put Alice in an awkward position.

Cameron going rogue was nothing new; he had a reputation for it. But at CamelCat Marketing he was usually the primary contributor of code, so things had a way of working themselves out. But now he was going rogue as a minority contributor, and everyone was suffering. Every step he attempted to take forward was, in fact, dragging the project *back* two steps. With only days to go until launch, it was not something that could be tolerated. Not right at the finish line. The stakes were too high.

The power dynamic between Alice and Cameron was uncomfortable. They both felt it. No longer the lead on his project, but technically the boss of the person who was, Cameron had authority over the project by proxy. So Alice knew she had to take a stand.

She delivered an ultimatum: 'Join the team efforts, in earnest, or lose access to the repo.'

Cameron scoffed at the threat, neither agreeing nor disagreeing to the terms. The emerging New Guard at CamelCat Marketing was not doing things in a way that made sense to him. But eventually, after another silent, inactive day, he toned down his rebellion and contributed to the project in a limited capacity without incident.

For launch day, Alice cleared everyone's schedule. If they weren't working on either deploying or testing the new code, they were working on the wrong thing. For at least a few hours, calls would go unanswered and e-mails would go unread. It required everyone's effort to get right.

As an upgrade to an existing system, [theoretically] the deployment would be simple. But it was far from guaranteed. They had been testing with production data, but only a recent slice of it.

The migration process in particular concerned Alice and Michael, as a number of changes to the database schemata had to be made. Many of the changes were simple enough, but the addition of indices was the big unknown. On a significantly large database, would the process of adding those indices cause problems? Would the database lock up and cause the application to stall? Would the server require far more memory than anyone had anticipated and simply fall over? No one knew.

Purple Budgie Finance had been warned to expect some fleeting performance issues for up to half an hour while the deployment was under way. On the happy path, the whole thing was expected to take less than a minute or two, so as long as they could quickly roll back, 30 minutes was plenty of time to cover the worst-case scenario.

When noon rolled around and the time came, everyone downed tools. The last major pieces of work had been completed the previous evening, and the morning had been spent mopping up bugs. Of which there were still many. But a work of art is never finished, and it was now or never.

Dru gathered the team to deliver a pep talk, the first since her ill-fated announcement that they were all doomed.

'I just want to thank each and every one of you for working so hard to get us to this point. A month ago I messed up, and a lot of you lost faith in me as your leader. Our company was in trouble, and I didn't have a plan. But you've all rallied around and pulled off the impossible to give us a fighting chance. I couldn't ask for a better group of people to work with, no matter what happens. Thank you for sticking with us and believing.'

The reaction was mixed, but heads were generally nodding. Something special had indeed occurred over the last few weeks.

Dru wiped a small tear from the corner of her eye. She grinned, pumped her fist in the air and yelled, 'Now let's launch this fucker!'

Applause broke out, and everyone rushed to their desks, ready to deal with whatever happened next.

Alice, Michael and Dru gathered around Michael's desk. Dru called Cameron over and asked, 'Would you like to do the honours?'

Cameron nodded, took Michael's mouse and clicked the *Deploy* button.

They waited.

CHAPTER 19
THE MOMENT OF TRUTH

THE BACK-END DEPLOYMENT was taking longer than expected. It was *not* going to be a one-minute process. But, at the five-minute mark, it was at least approaching its penultimate stage: database migrations.

The front-end deployment was a lot faster—around 20 seconds to spin up the build pipeline, ten seconds to build the front-end application, then a few seconds to push the build artefact, and invalidate the CDN cache.

The front-end pipeline kicked off, compiled the application, deployed it, and exited. Refreshing the browser showed that the front-end deployment had completed.

But the back-end deployment still had not.

It was what they had feared: the database migrations were taking longer than expected. Inspecting the logs, Michael could see that only the first of four migrations had finished executing.

Not a huge problem, if that was the benchmark. It was far from ideal, but fell within the deployment window they had promised to Purple Budgie Finance. If the production system was a bit sluggish during that time, that was to be expected.

Everyone's attention was glued to the deployment logs and the progress bar that crept along, one pixel at a time. They were focused on nothing else. Not least of all the phone in Dru's office, which had been ringing and falling through to voicemail. Calls and e-mails were, after all, not being dealt with right now. It was all hands on deck to support deployment and testing, the latter of which could kick off any second.

But someone was trying to get through, and before long Dru's mobile phone began to ring. One eye still on the deployment, she pulled out her phone and glanced at it. It was no longer ringing, but she had a message:

MONICA PB

Emergency! Pls pick up

Monica rang again, and Dru tapped to answer.

'Monica, hi. We're just releasing the update for you. What's up?'

The other side of the conversation was anyone's guess, but within moments Dru had grabbed Cameron's laptop and was attempting to log onto the CRM. It stalled, and an unhelpful error message greeted her.

Evelyn scooted over to check it out. They had warned of possible issues during the release window, so it wasn't the end of the world.

Right?

'I'll get it sorted straight away, don't worry. Thank you. Bye.' Dru ended the call. The other side of the conversation was still anyone's guess, but it didn't sound good.

'That was Monica,' Dru explained. 'She's um... she's at a conference, about to do a demo. And she needs the CRM.'

'Shit!' Evelyn muttered.

Cameron did not beat around the bush: 'Fucking clients, man.'

Alice sprang into action, warning: 'Cam, that's not helpful. We can bitch about this later down the pub. But right now, our client's about to embarrass themselves. This worked in UAT, so we need to find out what's gone wrong. Quickly.'

Cameron rolled his eyes and wandered down the other end of the office.

'I'm on it,' Michael said, taking over Cameron's laptop.

He pulled up the application logs and began searching for uncaught exceptions. There was nothing obvious. Separately, Evelyn and Robert attempted to replicate the issue. It did not take them long. The initial page would load, but login attempts failed with a generic error message.

In an average tech company, with an average application, most developers would have checked for console or network errors. But Evelyn knew it would not be that simple. The framework on which most of CamelCat Marketing's applications were built was old. It was old at the point she joined the company, and had been unmaintained by the community for a number of years. To say that it did not frequently emit errors would be a lie. A big one. Over the years, the framework had been hacked at to deal with most problems. Wacky workarounds were everywhere—a favourite trick was to set a timer to check that a variable had been populated, and kick off a corrective process if it remained in a null state for too long. To the user, it was a seamless—albeit slow—experience. But to developers? The code was pure spaghetti, and the errors too numerous to give any meaningful insight at a glance. They numbered in the hundreds. It would take hours to inspect them all.

'Is there anything that's failing *more* than usual?' Robert asked.

Evelyn snorted. 'I'm sure there is, but I'll be damned if I can find it.' She swivelled her chair towards Michael. 'What about on the back end? Any endpoints failing more often than usual?'

'Interesting thought,' he said.

He began to type in the terminal. Tailing the application logs, he grepped the output for all the usual suspects: 404s, 401s, 403s, 500s... He parsed the data into a CSV and loaded it up in a spreadsheet application. A quick graph revealed the largest offender.

'Bingo!' he exclaimed. 'There's a tonne of 404s.'

Alice threw her head back and grasped it in her hands.

Letting out a sigh, she asked: 'Is everything broken, or just one thing? We're still only halfway through these database migrations. I thought we built everything to be backwards compatible?'

'We did, I don't understand it,' Michael confirmed as he scrolled through the raw data.

'Anything?' Evelyn asked.

He continued scrolling, then announced: 'Aha! Looks like an endpoint that exchanges a refresh token for an access token.'

'Can we roll back?' Alice asked.

'Well... we *could*,' Michael answered.

'But?'

'But this stuck migration adds a wrinkle,' he explained. 'I'm just looking at the code now, and it looks like this is a new authentication method we're using. Once the back end finishes deploying, the old auth method—the one currently in production—will stop working. Rolling back the front end will fix it temporarily, but the second the back-end deploy finishes, it's broken again. When's Monica presenting?'

'Ten minutes from now,' Dru answered.

Michael shook his head. 'Yeah, that makes me nervous. The rate we're going, it'll break again right in the middle of her demo.'

'And we can't cancel the back-end deploy because the database is half-migrated...' Alice mused. 'What are our options? And why the hell did we change the authentication method? That wasn't part of Accelerate.'

By now, Cameron had returned. 'Is that my auth fix you're talking about?' he asked. 'Pretty neat, huh? I added it this morning. Can you believe we've been using Basic Auth this whole time while the framework actually has a built-in OAuth flow? It was super simple to enable. Just a few lines of code.'

The tension in the air was suddenly palpable. It was like Oscar was stood there, raging. But instead, it was Alice.

'Cameron,' she asked calmly, 'does your OAuth flow require a database migration in order to work?'

'Yeah, of course,' he answered.

She closed her eyes and shook her head.

'Please tell me you weren't exaggerating about the simplicity of that change. Was it really just a few lines?'

Cameron nodded. 'Sure. Like I said: low-hanging fruit.'

Alice took a deep breath, plastered on her most convincing smile, and turned to face the team.

'Okay, so here's the plan. Someone quickly revert the auth flow on the front end. Find out what the code used to look like, then put it in a try/catch with the new code. Deploy it straight away, then everyone jump on testing. Just click through everything and look for anything else that's broken.'

'Will this solve the problem for Monica?' Dru asked.

Alice nodded. 'If we act quickly.'

'In that case...' Dru pulled out her purse and waved it in the air. 'Pizza on me if we're testing in the next five minutes!'

While the developers applied the fix, Alice beckoned Cameron to join her out of earshot of the others.

'Damn it Cameron, why can't you just be happy colouring inside the lines? Everyone's trying to move Heaven and Earth to get this thing done; why did you have to build in something we didn't need? And right at the finish line?!'

Cameron did not respond. He stared at her, unflinching. And Alice, in turn, stared back. They were toe-to-toe and eye-to-eye. Alice had never been so vocal, and Cameron never so threatened. The New Guard was coming.

EPILOGUE

MONICA STEPPED ON STAGE, loaded the CRM, and attempted to log in. Behind her, her laptop screen was projected ten feet tall, visible to everyone in attendance.

'Well, that's embarrassing,' she commented, as the login error displayed. 'Hotel wifi, am I right?' she joked.

She tried a few more times.

On the fourth attempt, the login was successful, and the presentation began.

———

The deployment was eventually a success. In testing, two minor bugs surfaced. One was patched and deployed within minutes, but the other was trickier to get to the bottom of. It affected an obscure part of the system, so the team collectively decided to capture the bug in a ticket and accept the risk.

The day that had peaked with a bang went out with a whimper. Traffic began to flow to the CRM's new features, and spot checking suggested that the recommendations being generated were sound.

At the end of the week, Robert and Evelyn celebrated their last day with the company. Over a pub lunch, the conversation turned to Alice's model, which had allowed the team to quickly pivot and deliver a solution that solved the client's core requirements without sinking time into excessive *nice to haves.*

Cameron was uncharacteristically quiet. As the others celebrated a technique that he had not championed—that had literally reversed some of his proudest work—he contemplated his career.

That weekend he asked Dru to join him for coffee and informed her of his intention to step down from the company they had created together. Sure that he had been onto something, he wanted to do some consulting work to support himself whilst working on a new machine learning startup.

It was a tough moment. They had their problems, and Dru had certainly not forgotten his recent actions, but they had been through a lot together. And, contrary to however their relationship presented to the outside world, they were close friends. They had met during university at a pub quiz and bonded over 70s music trivia. Some time later CamelCat Marketing was born of a drunken whiteboarding session after a final year party.

To fill the vacancy at the top of the development team, Alice was asked to step in as interim Head of Engineering. She accepted for a fixed term of six months.

When a full-time CTO came onboard, Alice declined an offer to remain in management, insisting on rejoining the development team as an individual contributor.

Michael had been convinced to stay on a permanent basis, and after a long search a front-end lead was also due to come on board.

Under Alice's watch, the team retained the Purple Budgie Finance contract, and wowed two new clients with insightful project executions. They even managed to cull dozens of unused features from a variety of legacy projects, saving countless person-hours in maintenance.

The business was still on life support, but it had survived to fight another day.

UNDERSTANDING THE MODEL

OVERVIEW

THE PARABLE YOU have just read is one of missed opportunities and misaligned priorities. The cast of characters spans the idealist, the brilliant jerk, the chancer, and the recovering burn-out, among many others.

The story itself may sound familiar. At some point, most professionals will have worked on similar projects, with looming deadlines, severe consequences, and lack of proper communication.

The principles embodied and processes employed at all stages of the parable are likewise nothing new. They should feel familiar to anyone who has worked in a handful of teams.

Alice's model is somewhat secondary to the best practices it prompts. Its purpose is to help teams adopt those best practices by requiring them to ask questions that cannot be answered without first engaging in iterative work, close collaboration with stakeholders, critical assessment of successes and failures, and a willingness to be humble inside a blameless culture.

On the surface, the model asks two simple questions: *Is a solution used?* and *Was the solution requested?*

It may seem that the questions are so simple they do not need to be asked; it is usually obvious when a developer goes rogue and builds something fantastical that they have not been asked to, and common sense likewise dictates that you should only build the things that will be used.

But the simplicity is deceiving.

If we take a solution at face value, we could very easily conclude that, because a customer literally asked for it, and we see from logs that they are using it, that it was the right thing to build. But when we look closer, we may discover that this is not quite the case.

Perhaps a solution generates reports, on which the customer then carries out hours of manual tweaking and post-processing before they can be presented to stakeholders. That essential, offline work is impossible to capture in logs.

Or perhaps the solution is *never* used, as the person who commissioned it had no direct experience of the problem it was intended to solve. They may have shared an idealised or less-than-factual account of their organisational challenges that, ultimately, fell short of prompting a workable solution.

In using the model, the real task is, therefore, to plot a solution and observe which quadrant you *think* it fits into, and then critically assess your core assumptions about *why*. In some cases your first assessment will be accurate, but very often it will not, and from there you can begin to reprioritise.

It is almost always necessary to measure and iterate on solutions to determine the answer to the question, *do they use it?* This applies both during development (at what point do beta testers give up?) and after launch (how efficiently is it being used?).

This is what brought success to CamelCat Marketing as their deadline approached: when their software development lifecycle began to include daily side-by-side tests, comparisons against the incumbent solution, and iterations incorporating the resultant insights.

When measuring and iterating, some solutions may emerge as candidates to be dropped, whereas others may emerge as candidates to double down on.

The chapters that follow look at each of the model's quadrants, focusing on assumptions we might make about the solutions that fall into them, and ways in which a solution may actually belong to another quadrant altogether.

Though not exhaustive, it should provide a good starting point for critically assessing the solutions you work on, helping to avoid the traps that yield the least rewards, double down on the solutions that will delight your users, and blamelessly cut your losses where mistakes were made.

MISSION CRITICAL

WHEN BUILDING SOLUTIONS, the majority should be those that are Mission Critical. They are the solutions that people have both asked for and are using.

Let's look at a couple of examples.

If your business is a digital agency like CamelCat Marketing, much of your work will involve creating websites for clients. Providing a content management system (CMS) to subsequently manage those websites would likely be considered a Mission Critical solution, as web content is rarely static.

Alternatively, if your business designs point of sale (POS) devices, an LCD screen to display the transaction price to both customers and merchants—arguably bare-minimum functionality for such a device—would be Mission Critical to ensure transactions are not under- or over-charged.

These are the kinds of solutions that exist at the intersection of *what users ask for* and *what users use*. They are obvious, essential pieces of functionality that may even define the entire product.

Mission Critical status is the positive end state of any

solution. Just as businesses settle from being volatile and unproven entities into stable, reliable machines, so too should solutions. (The danger of complacency in this position is something we will touch on later.)

BUILDING WHAT IS OBVIOUS

Building what is obvious will help to secure your place in the market. It is the CMS in your website, the steering wheel in your car, and the protein in your burger.

Certain solutions define products and services, and these are usually the easiest to decide to build.

If you are starting a new product or business, it is these solutions that you will want to focus on. They will not get you to a place of outsize success on their own—if they are obvious to *you*, they will also be obvious to your competitors—but whatever else makes your offering special cannot exist without that which is first Mission Critical. You will always need a boring, solid foundation on which to build exciting things.

Let's explore this further, with a couple of examples of fictional businesses whose overall solutions misfire by the omission of one small, Mission Critical detail.

First consider a publishing company that specialises in literature covering geography and world politics. They prepare a new educational textbook for school children that includes a page on each of the world's countries. At the back of the book are challenges for the students, including one that involves naming countries by their flags. This *could* be a fun activity facilitated by the book, or it *could* be an impossible task, depending on how the publisher has the book printed. To help keep printing costs low—because the historic margin on similar books has been low—they opt for the cheapest printing methods. When the books arrive in schools, they superficially appear to be fit for purpose: the text is legible, and all the pages are there. But six months into the school term a problem occurs: one of the cost-cutting measures was to print the textbooks in black and white, and some flags—such as those belonging to Norway and Iceland—look very similar in a greyscale palette. Marking the children's tests using the answer sheet that accompanied the textbooks, teachers do not notice the issue, and the pass rate for affected questions is half what it should have been. The Mission Critical solution that was overlooked was the use of colour.

Now consider a decorator who takes on a job to paint a ground-floor room that has become grubby and stained over the years. They choose a premium quality paint, put down sheets and plastic coverings, and work diligently all day. The following day they return to apply a second layer. Following their efforts, the room is a brilliant white. Then, after a few weeks, a water stain begins to appear on the ceiling, at the site of an old leak. The missing Mission Critical part of the process was the application of a stain blocker prior to painting. Now, as the rest of the ceiling is a brilliant white, the old stain will appear even more conspicuous than before.

In both of these examples, one very simple, very minor addition would have made all the difference.

Without those tiny, essential details, the solution as a whole is not fit for purpose. And if you do not deliver on the basics, people are not likely to rely on you to provide future solutions for their needs.

The same, of course, applies when developing software applications.

If you build a website for a client without an accompanying CMS, you will not have a happy client. The thing you have delivered may technically work—users can visit the website, and you will happily take on amendments for the client as another paid project—but you will have subverted their expectation of what constitutes a website in the 21st century.

By failing to build the obvious, your solution will not hold its own on any level against its competitors, and you will not gain a reputation as an obvious choice of vendor.

LEARNING FROM THE PAST

Sometimes, it is not obvious what will work. Particularly if what you are attempting to create is something entirely new to the world.

We take the obvious things for granted. Automobile manufacture, bakery, and house building are industries with an established way of doing things. They have an agreed set of solutions and ways of working that are obvious: a car requires a braking system, houses need insulation, etc.

But what happens when an industry is not mature enough to have established, tried-and-tested norms? An industry such as software development, for example? In a fast-moving industry that is still in the throes of discovering itself and reflecting on the long-term efficacy of its emergent standards and best practices, it can be difficult to know instinctively what to build, especially when it comes to disrupting another industry with this new, unproven technology. Will our great ideas become the next big thing, or will they be a passing fad that time will reveal to have been completely useless?

In such circumstances, it can help to look to previous projects. Our collective memory and learnings may be few, but we should still aim to draw on them where they do exist. One success or failure does not a pattern make, but we will only be able to establish those long-term patterns by repeating what has come before and observing over time how it all shakes out.

Think back to a project in which you had either significant

authority or visibility of outcomes and ask, *What worked well and what did not?*

What was the one decision or solution that everyone bought into that, in hindsight, turned out to be a mistake? Perhaps your team made the same mistake as Cameron and decided to adopt a shiny new piece of technology whose utility was based primarily on hype? Or perhaps you based your entire platform around an immature database management system (DBMS) that turned out to lose data at scale?

Or—not to just focus on the negative—was there something you put your faith in that turned out to be a roaring success?

Whatever the case, you can use this kind of retrospective as a guide on what to build (and, perhaps more importantly, what *not* to build): from the highest-level initiative through to the smallest implementation detail.

It may not always provide a clear path to success, but the more the path is trodden the more (or less!) likely you will tread it again.

UNDERSTANDING THE PROBLEM

When it comes to understanding the frustrations *caused* by a problem, being one of those who *experiences* the problem goes a long way.

But we are not always so lucky.

If you find yourself a mere cog in a machine, you will not understand the mission like the lone founder who is desperate to improve some element of life for people like themselves.

So talking to those who will use the solution is a must.

When Alice spoke to Oscar, she asked questions that went far beyond what the solution was expected to *be*. She delved into what problem was being solved, and then went even further to understand where the existing solution fell short. Stripping back all assumptions, Oscar's ideal was a system that would allow him to minimise the human effort needed to run his existing solution. When thinking and speaking at that level, he did not mention any specific technology or methodology.

The *why* of the until-then accepted solution was that machine learning could replicate the human portion of a job that was no longer scalable with humans, and that machines could be infinitely scaled. However, it missed the opportunity afforded by questioning the premise of *why* that was even a suitable solution in the first place.

Upon closer inspection, Alice discovered that the part of the system everyone assumed must be replaced was not even the correct area in which to focus. Although *replacing humans* was the driving force of the project, it soon became apparent that humans (and their particular skills) were not a hard requirement: manipulating spreadsheets to transform data was unnecessary if the customer relationship management (CRM) tool boasted a slightly enhanced sorting and filtering solution; and the assumption that advanced pattern matching was even required turned out to be false.

CHALLENGING ASSUMPTIONS

The old ways are the best. A common refrain, and not difficult to believe. The old ways are tried and tested; they are familiar; they are often easy.

But they can also be limiting if they prevent us from daring to dream. And to dream, you must challenge assumptions.

Question, as Alice did, how well an existing solution actually works. If it can be described by no better word than *satisfactory*, there may be room to innovate a better solution.

Consider buildings. Skyscrapers stretch to unbelievable heights, bear immense weight, and withstand whatever turbulence the air and ground can throw at them. Some modern innovations have increased the height to which we can build, but the underlying principles have remained unchanged. The cathedrals of Europe and the pyramids of multiple, disparate cultures have survived hundreds and thousands of years, respectively—fairly conclusive proof that those methods of construction are fit for purpose.

In contrast, consider medicine. Modern medicine is miraculous. Diseases that have plagued humanity for thousands of years are manageable, treatable, and in some cases eradicated. But it was not always so. While the epic cathedrals of the Renaissance were being ably constructed, bloodletting and trepanning were commonplace treatments for a variety of ailments. These practices persisted as no better solutions were available. Then, in a relatively short period of time, antibiotics, sterilisation of equipment, and vaccines emerged, changing everything.

Building methods have remained relatively stable because they have consistently solved their problem exceptionally well. Medicine has pivoted dramatically as its problem has not been solved well enough, often enough.

Those are, of course, simple examples. It's rarely so easy to tell; hindsight is a wonderful thing.

No matter how established your industry, you cannot know for certain whether the received wisdom that drives your ways of working is sound and efficient, or whether you are steeped in dogma from what will come to be known as your industry's dark ages. Not knowing what you do not know is the beginning of wisdom, but it is also a tremendous blocker for progress.

As the saying often—and likely incorrectly—attributed to Henry Ford goes:

> If I had asked people what they wanted, they would have said *faster horses*.

It is difficult to instinctively know what a better alternative might look like. The owner of a retail website (where 2% of visitors are typically converted into paying customers) might delight at a 5% conversion rate. But what if a highly effective, targeted marketing strategy resulted in a majority of visitors who were ready to purchase? Suddenly, a 50% conversion rate may feel more appropriate. But until you know the *50%* option exists, the 5% option sounds very attractive.

A better solution doesn't have to be revolutionary in design; it can instead be revolutionary in its simplicity. For CamelCat Marketing, the most elegant solution ended up being a simple extension to an existing system. Such a boring solution was not at all obvious. And this is the nature of received wisdom: it seems obvious.

It can be pervasive. A single piece of received wisdom can be thousands of years old, and so fundamental to our understanding of the world that we no longer recognise its presence. It is like the smell of our home, to which we are noseblind, but to which guests are acutely aware. Familiarity begets invisibility. It is the reason we have to prompt ourselves to 'think outside the box'.

So when we take the time to dispose of our preconceptions, we can discover alternatives. And from there, we can discover better ways to deliver the Mission Critical.

The decision makers at CamelCat Marketing and Purple Budgie Finance had multiple options available to them, but were led by assumptions. It took only a little effort to uncover a better solution.

We must remember not to take our assumptions for granted. There may be a better way.

BURNING DOWN THE CASTLE

It is all fine and well to question received wisdom and dig into problems at the ideation stage, but what happens when a solution is already underway? Or when the task at hand is to fix or build upon something that already exists?

The question we must ask ourselves is: *What would happen if I just got rid of this?*

It is the question Alice asked of the work on Project Accelerate.

It is a tough call to make. Especially when significant time, effort and money have been spent. Far too often, project leaders will default to proceeding with poor implementations of Mission Critical solutions because of the sunk-cost fallacy, just hoping against hope that it will all somehow work out in the end (more on this later).

Whether you intend to try something new, or give up entirely, the first step is to stop and take stock of the situation, before burning it all to the ground.

You may find it useful to imagine that the project has *already* burned down, through some circumstance in which you are blameless. In such a situation, what opportunities for rebuilding would excite you?

Consider the evolution of how humans share knowledge.

The advent of written communication changed the world. Knowledge could be passed down through generations without the need for oral storytelling and the diminished accuracy introduced by each retelling. The written word allowed religious texts, laws, and general knowledge to be documented in a static medium, as accurate a century down the line as the day they were written.

So powerful a tool was writing that someone who did not know how to read or write could inherit a document written by a great-grandparent, meticulously copy the shapes they saw onto a new piece of paper, then pass it on to a great-grandchild and burn the original. The descendent could obtain the knowledge of their great-great-great-great-grandparent, even if none of the intervening generations were able to read or write.

Making copies of culturally important texts was a no-brainer. It was Mission Critical to society, for the advancements it enabled and the knowledge it preserved.

And with such a powerful, important, tried-and-tested way of preserving knowledge, how hard would most people think about finding a replacement? Yes, manually copying texts was time-consuming, but the benefits of doing so were immense. It was more than a fair trade.

Enter Johannes Gutenberg, who in 1440 created the printing press and revolutionised the transfer of knowledge. Recreating documents became cheap, fast, and accurate. If the written word was powerful before, Gutenberg's innovation took it to a whole new level.

The status quo made *so much* sense, until someone dared to challenge it and ask whether things could be even better. The inefficiencies of the old method—tolerated literally since records began because of the sheer utility it yielded—became largely abandoned in favour of a new, standard, Mission Critical solution.

This is what Alice did when she questioned the intent of Project Accelerate. The work in progress had the potential to provide a solution, but it was merely a digital analogue of an existing approach that provided results not *because of* its methods, but *in spite of* them. As with manually copying documents, Oscar's spreadsheet was bottlenecked by the capacity of humans to manipulate data. The benefit of the proposed machine learning solution was primarily to speed up the original steps. And why not? The status quo is powerful, especially when it yields favourable results.

Challenging every assumption about how to solve the problem, Alice abandoned an unnecessarily complex and challenging idea, and burned it all down to start again with something not only faster, but also simpler, and more efficient.

No looking back.

———

FOOD FOR THOUGHT: EVERYTHING'S A SPREADSHEET

Have you ever noticed that the majority of software projects essentially boil down to recreating spreadsheets on the Web?

Sometimes the UI is nice and polished, but the underlying business logic is usually identical to whatever spreadsheet was previously responsible for doing the job.

Look for the underlying spreadsheets (sometimes literal, sometimes figurative); you'll find them everywhere. And ask the question: Is there an opportunity to rethink the logic when migrating away from them?

STROKE OF GENIUS

SOME SOLUTIONS CHANGE how people think about a product, or even an industry. They are based on disruptive ideas that are so breathtakingly obvious it is difficult to understand why no one had come up with them before.

Solutions that are a Stroke of Genius are not always the bread and butter of a product, but they can set the direction of it and its competitors for decades to come.

There are typically two types of Stroke of Genius: those ideas that change the world, and those that change an industry.

Most of us will never accomplish the former, but it can still be helpful to understand what falls into that category. Ideas as ancient as the Wheel and as recent as the Internet qualify.

What sets them apart is what they *enable*: specifically, that they enable the second kind of Stroke of Genius.

With widespread adoption of the Wheel, large-scale building projects became less labour-intensive. [Mass] transit also became, for the first time in history, not only possible but a part of daily life, with carts, trains, and cars taking individuals and groups from *A* to *B* with ease.

In modern times, the Internet has enabled similar efficiencies. Where we would once have to wait weeks to see holiday photos, and were limited to purchasing whatever products were sold by local merchants, now we can see—and delete!—our photographs in real time (and as a part of our daily lives, not just when on holiday), and shop from most of the world's merchants. And those local merchants have gained the ability to sell their products the world over.

A few other industries that have been disrupted by adoption of the Internet include banking, music, and television/film. In fact, you may be hard-pressed to find an industry that has not, in some way, been disrupted in recent years. Each of those disruptions started with a Stroke of Genius.

But a Stroke of Genius does not have to turn your entire industry on its head; it can also be a small thing that sets you apart from your competitors.

With a superior user experience disrupting just a small part of your industry, you can increase your market share to the point where your Stroke of Genius becomes a piece of Mission Critical functionality that all of your competitors have copied and maybe even improved upon.

It is these ideas that we will now explore.

HAVING A WONDERFUL INSIGHT

The purest form of a Stroke of Genius is having a wonderful insight into an unsolved human frustration that has not yet been capitalised upon.

Though it may seem a trivial example, we can look at the audio and video cassettes that experienced their heyday in the 1980s.

Magnetic tapes as an audiovisual storage medium were a game changer for home consumption of music, film, and television shows. And there was one particular piece of functionality that emerged to make the technology even easier to use: the ability for VCRs and cassette players to detect the end of the tape and either play the other side or initiate the rewind operation.

Both actions traditionally required manual intervention. In the case of turning over a cassette, the cost to the listener was disruption of their groove (a particular problem when listening to lengthy concept albums). And in the case of having to rewind at the end of a tape, there was a very real familial and societal pressure to rewind as a matter of courtesy (and a degree of shame assigned if you did not).

When the companies manufacturing these machines realised that they could eliminate those frustrations with mechanisms that would remove the need for human interaction, that was a wonderful insight. No longer would music fans be snapped out of their trance after the climax of The Great Gig In The Sky.

It is a simple, silly thing when viewed through a modern lens. But at the time was a very welcome feature. And when comparing options in store, those without such a feature were less likely to be purchased.

Eventually, consumer pressure meant that the solution became commonplace, available in models at all price points. It graduated from a Stroke of Genius to an obvious, asked-for, and used Mission Critical solution in its own right.

BEING AHEAD OF YOUR TIME

You may have an unrealised Stroke of Genius on your hands that you are certain will eventually become Mission Critical. But it is not guaranteed. Sometimes, you may be too early to the party.

When innovating, you don't *just* have to get the solution right; you also have to get the timing right.

A 2010s smartphone would not have been warmly received in the 1980s. Without accompanying concepts such as social networking and on-demand media, it would likely have been received as a useless science fiction fad reserved solely for the world's nerds.

So be prepared for the possibility that the game-changing idea that you are certain will revolutionise the world may in fact fall flat on its face and become a textbook Waste of Time, only to become a wildly successful Stroke of Genius under someone else's watch a decade or so later.

It always pays to be aware of what cultural norms your genius idea will be fighting against. No matter how small the idea, it will pose a challenge to how things have always been done. In some industries, this disruption may seek to upend traditions and norms that have been in place for years, decades, centuries, or even millennia.

Suppose you manage to develop a new method of raising children. Something that you are able to conclusively show, beyond any reasonable doubt, is more effective than any other methodology. How do you think that would go down with the world's parents?

The most significant challenge to gaining widespread adoption would not relate to the proven benefits of your new method, but instead to the implications that come with it. Specifically, that if your method is so much better than the alternatives, those alternatives are now sub-par. Alternatives that may have been used throughout all of human history. Alternative that parents have already raised children with.

It is a very human thing to not wish to be proven wrong, or made to feel inadequate or foolish. So without first winning over the hearts and minds of those that will benefit from your Stroke of Genius, you may risk alienating the very people that your solution aims to improve the lives of.

We see this in the modern day when it comes to the education system. Traditional mass schooling was established during the Industrial Revolution, in a time when children were being prepared for a life on the factory floor, and creativity and critical thinking were not requirements for the vast majority of work. In this scenario, facing forward to engage in rote learning was effective.

With the rise of modern technology and the jobs that have come with it, this is no longer the case. Yet the layout of the classroom and the structure of lessons has remained largely unchanged for over a hundred years—children are still schooled in the art of memorisation to pass exams, not on skills that are *actually* required in the workplace or their adult lives.

And it makes sense why an outdated model that everyone has been subjected to persists. When attempts are made to take a greenfield approach to education—especially when supported by studies—the implication is clear: the way you were taught as a child is wrong, the way you are teaching and have taught your own children is wrong, and a significant chunk of your youth and formative years were wasted, never to be reclaimed.

And the implication for educators is even worse: those educated, intelligent people who have dedicated their lives to helping children may actually be doing more harm than good.

That's a tough emotional obstacle to overcome. How receptive would *you* be to that kind of feedback?

We see a similar issue with the slow adoption of electric cars in the early 21st century. Much of the marketing and logic for buying an electric vehicle is centred around the damage caused to the planet by fossil-fuel-powered vehicles. The implication being that everyone has actively spent a significant chunk of their life and earnings killing the planet.

Not a good way to win people over.

It is not because people are bad that they are so reluctant to embrace an objectively better option, but because they do not take kindly to being told that they have been doing things wrong, merely for embracing the only option that was made available to them.

In fighting to save your Stroke of Genius from becoming a Waste of Time, being able to maintain the intensity of your message whilst also approaching your audience with empathy is your biggest challenge.

It may, therefore, be a very slow journey from ideation to adoption. And as you build towards adoption, you should constantly assess not only your likelihood for success, but also your appetite (and / or ability) to carry on in light of those odds.

NOT UNDERSTANDING THE USERS' REQUIREMENTS

In pursuing a Stroke of Genius, you must be sure that you have adequately understood the underlying problem that you are attempting to solve—it is easy to get carried away with an attractive idea that only superficially solves the problem you have been tasked with.

Suppose a client states they need a tool to help them 'reach people'. You diligently research their business, conduct interviews with their target audience, and understand all there is to be understood about how those individuals traditionally interact with such a company.

You build a clever mass-mailing feature into your product, with an easy-to-use WYSIWYG editor, hook it up to a print and mailing service, and reveal your Stroke of Genius combination of services to the client, expecting praise and fanfare.

Instead, you hear crickets.

Your client did not require a way to physically communicate with potential customers. Their real problem was a lack of engagement relative to the money spent on their advertising campaigns. In asking for a way to 'reach people', they were really searching for a way to emotionally connect with potential customers.

With all the best intentions in the world, you have unwittingly created a genius service that no one asked for. It is a case where a supposed Stroke of Genius is: on your part, actually Vision ≠ Reality; and on the client's part, a Waste of Time. Far too often, well-intentioned folk get carried away solutionising, having heard only the briefest description of a problem.

You must always understand the requirements you are building for. This does not mean you have to obtain a fully formed plan from your clients or users. But it does mean that you should understand the problem that you are attempting to solve, in plain, unambiguous terms.

If in doubt, explain your understanding of the problem, in your own words, to a third-party—ideally someone outside of the industry entirely, who knows as little as possible about your respective businesses, is unfamiliar with the problem, and is oblivious to any of your shared jargon. And then ask them to describe the problem to you in their own words. Does everyone have the same understanding of the problem? If not, you will need to dig deeper.

ONE STEP AT A TIME

The tricky thing about a Stroke of Genius is that, regardless of how obvious it may appear to you, its actual success will not likely become self-evident for some time.

So you must be realistic with your approach to building brand new things. It would be a terrible waste of your time, money, and energy to dedicate your life to building something that the world is not yet ready for. However, that should not discourage you from trying; you merely need to be focused and willing to iterate on the solution.

Your *big* idea might be something that you only realise at the very end of your career, having built dozens of products in dozens of companies, all related in some way to your magnum opus, and all gradually laying the groundwork for its eventual mass acceptance.

Consider rocketry: if we were able to travel back in time and provide rocket technology to the Romans, they would likely not think of it as a means to reach Mars, nor would they consider space tourism or communication satellites. In their world, the technology would be directly applicable instead to weaponry—such weapons, of course, being the genesis of the field of rocketry, starting with the invention gunpowder in Imperial China.

If your Stroke of Genius shows early signs of interest, but not in the way you had anticipated, you have three options: continue as planned; abandon it as a failed experiment, or; pivot into what users want.

Continuing with the solution as planned is fraught with risk. There is no guarantee that you will be successful in gaining widespread acceptance and adoption of your idea, and one of the best-case scenarios is that, in decades to come, people look back fondly on what you tried to do, remarking, 'That was really ahead of its time.'

Going in entirely the opposite direction, you could abandon the idea as a failed experiment. This is not the worst possible course of action, but you should ensure your early feedback demonstrates a complete lack of appetite for what you are *really* trying to do; you want to be sure you really were barking up the wrong tree. If this describes your solution, then recognising it as a Waste of Time and killing it may be a wise decision. You can always revisit it at a later date when you believe attitudes have shifted.

The third option, however, may provide you with the greatest chance of success. It is the option that much of the tech industry is based upon, and needs very little explanation: build a little, solicit feedback, pivot where necessary, build some more. If your idea has even a tiny amount of traction, you can follow the breadcrumbs laid out by your users until you have built something that has a decent level of adoption.

This allows you to achieve two things.

The first is that you will have built a Mission Critical solution, by: listening to what your users, clients, or customers are saying; collecting data, and; building something appropriate.

The second is that you will have built at least a small part of your Stroke of Genius, and put it out into the world.

Some of the greatest innovations took a long time to catch on precisely because they challenged the status quo and upended tradition. In the case of software, it may be the case that you need to wait five or more years until a new generation of users—uninhibited by the old way of doing things—come onto the scene as new individuals with purchasing power. Or, in the case of things that affect the whole of society, your task might be to change public perception one project at a time, until decades have passed and the demographics with purchasing power (typically: newer generations) have long been exposed to your way of thinking, priming someone else to take the mantle and deliver on your actual vision after you are gone.

We see this in the mission to improve public health and human longevity with efforts to shift to electric vehicles, eliminate the smoking of tobacco, and embrace sustainable, insect-based diets. Big change comes little by little, and typically fails if attempts are made to rush it.

If you do not have a grand plan to change the world, you can still iterate on what you are building if it is unproven. The iteration process itself plays a vital role in triaging an idea, helping you to commit the absolute minimum of time to building something before deciding whether to go all in or to cut your losses. You won't win them all, but you don't have to spend unnecessary time on something that is doomed to become a Waste of Time.

DOGFOODING TO TEST YOUR HYPOTHESES

The term *dogfooding* refers to the practice of *eating your own dogfood*, or, if that sounds disgusting, *using your own solutions*. This is a way to validate your ideas as you iterate on them.

If the solution you are building is in any way usable inside your own company, get as many people as possible to use it. Even better if you are building an internal solution and the staff that will be using it are different to those that are building it.

Any decrease in productivity that your company suffers as a result of such alpha testing will likely be greatly offset by the time you do not spend futilely chasing the wrong solutions.

CHECKING YOUR ASSUMPTIONS

Finally, it is worth critically examining the very premise of what you plan to build.

If you are classifying a solution as a Stroke of Genius, you may assume that it is a new idea. Depending on how litigious your mind (or company's solicitors) are, you may have even done your homework to establish that the genius idea you are contemplating really is brand new.

But a lack of easily identifiable prior art may also serve as a warning.

We live in a society where we assume that knowledge and information, once created, will exist forever. But the truth is that the information we create only persists as long as the tech company that is hosting that information stays not only in business, but in exactly the business of hosting that particular kind of information.

Furthermore, the tools at our disposal for discovering documents (search engines, at the time of writing) do a very good job of pruning missing and stale information from their indices.

Historically, important documents the world over have been recorded and stored on vellum, a material that has proven its longevity to last into millennia. The same cannot be said for modern modes of data storage. In just 20 years, between 2000 and 2020, the archival storage format of choice for consumers has rapidly switched from floppy disks, to CDs, to DVDs, to USB sticks, to cloud storage. At the time of writing, manufacturers largely no longer produce floppy disks, and the trend in modern devices is to not include any of the drives (and often none of the ports) required to interface with any of the physical storage items listed above.

In a time that roundly feels like a digital renaissance, we are quite likely actually in the middle of a dark age, with information saved forever in formats that will fall out of fashion, on media that is no longer produced, and held by companies that, in the grand scheme of things, are very new, often charge nothing (and, as is reasonable, promise nothing) for the data storage services they provide, and have not yet faced the test of time.

All of that is a long way to say that, if you cannot find evidence of prior art, that is not necessarily an indication that you have a brand new, world-changing idea. It *may* simply be the case that your idea has been tried before and failed at the earliest stages, before it was able to leave any kind of easily discoverable, enduring paper trail.

This poses an interesting challenge: how to measure the likelihood that you are repeating past mistakes when, by their very nature, evidence of them is difficult or even impossible to find?

VISION ≠ REALITY

IT IS OFTEN the case that much of the time we spend on what we *think* is Mission Critical work is, in fact, spent building solutions where Vision ≠ Reality. This is what happens when our information is incomplete, or our assumptions are misguided.

We saw how Cameron and Oscar believed machine learning to be a Mission Critical solution, even though Alice was able to show that a much simpler solution could achieve results with a reduced overhead and a higher level of accuracy.

When building something, it is not only important to ensure that we have a thorough, up-to-date understanding of the requirements—of the problem to be solved—but also that we are not precious about the work we have already carried out.

When things go wrong, it is easy to succumb to the sunk-cost fallacy and follow a Vision ≠ Reality solution through to completion simply because the thought of backtracking feels a bit too much like failure.

BUILDING ACCORDING TO PLAN

As humans, we have a strong survival instinct; the part of us that optimises our actions for obtaining and retaining shelter, warmth, and nourishment. Living in post-industrial societies, we obtain these things by holding down jobs that do not *directly* produce the means of survival, but instead provide us with the money to *buy* them.

Our jobs, therefore, become a proxy for survival.

How do you feel when you think about losing your job? The rational part of your brain knows that you can get another one, maybe even within a matter of days. But the animalistic part of your brain goes into panic mode. Strong, capable individuals can be reduced to tears upon learning that they have lost their job— the fact that they may immediately bounce back is no consolation, because the certainty that they can stay dry, warm, and nourished is temporarily lost.

In the workplace, this primal concern manifests as a strong desire to have a formal plan of action guiding our work. If we are told in clear terms *exactly* what it is that we are expected to do, we can demand to be measured not against the company's successes and failures, but by how well we played the role assigned to us. Our ability to survive stays within our control.

The employees of CamelCat Marketing could have been forgiven for thinking, *The project has failed and the company is facing financial difficulty, but I did exactly what I was asked, so if there are redundancies, I shouldn't be one of them.*

It is an understandable position, rooted in fairness. And the real problem occurs when that sentiment is felt not just by those doing the real work on the ground floor, but also by those who direct them, and those who direct *them*, all the way up to the top decision makers. When the very human desire to remain safe prompts *everyone* to adopt a way of working that protects their own interests even in failure, the likelihood of failure increases.

A software house may be contracted to deliver a piece of bespoke software for a fixed amount of money, within a fixed amount of time. A specification of some description will be provided—often a list of features—and work will commence, with a client demo scheduled for the week before launch. The demo will invariably be a disaster, with the client flabbergasted at how much essential functionality is missing.

Dru witnessed this when Oscar paid his first surprise visit to the CamelCat Marketing office. It was a situation created [in part] by Cameron's vague description to the team of what exactly they would be building; that the new dashboard would do 'all kinds of cool things'.

When building something new, there should be no surprises. No ambiguous specifications, no all-or-nothing client demos. Internal and external stakeholders should be equal partners in the development lifecycle, with a clear understanding of what is expected from them, and what they can expect in return.

It is an ongoing collaboration, and requires abandoning the comforting notion of a single, unchanging plan. It takes bravery.

If that bravery isn't forthcoming, you may find that you drift into a situation—often when time or money is about to run out—where it seems too late in the game to go back and fix *anything*. And then what happens? Everyone doubles down on the failing process, completes their small part of it to the letter, and blames everyone else when the end result is disappointing.

The developers point out that they have merely built what they were told; that all the company gave them was a bullet-pointed list of features. The project manager insists that the list came straight from the client's mouth, and that the developers failed to correctly expand those bullet points into workable solutions. The account manager blames everyone for making a mess of the project they worked so hard to win.

Who *technically* is at fault doesn't matter. What does matter is that everyone is acting in the spirit of self-preservation, and as a result the opportunity is lost to admit that mistakes were made, and to actually fix some of them.

There are really just two options. Either: everyone collectively agrees to continue tanking the project in hopes of protecting themselves, or; everyone can swallow their pride, get their heads out the sand, abandon the list, work closely with the customer to understand where the misalignment came from, and accept that there is more to be gained in the long run by delivering something that solves at least some of the problem well.

It is a scary process, because it involves admitting that you do not know exactly how a solution should work. But, practiced consistently, it will result in more successful solutions that, in turn, will result in more safety for all involved. If you can just ignore your lizard brain.

FORGETTING WHAT IS IMPORTANT

When building a product specification, it is not uncommon to have a set of *wish list* items: nice-to-have features or methodologies that are often rather exciting, but which do not solve the core problem on their own.

It is important to not allow such work to sneak off your wish list when the main body of work has not yet been successfully completed.

Sometimes that is easier said than done.

Consider timekeeping.

You might buy a watch to ensure that you make it to work on time every day. A hard requirement of such a timepiece is that it can accurately tell the time. For this, you need hands or a digital display. A date complication may also be useful if you work irregular shifts. If you don't want to risk being late because the watch has stopped, a solar-powered mechanism could be warranted. And if you are a fashion-conscious individual, a fancy brand name on the dial and small diamonds at the hour markers will show off your style.

But how many of those features were really important?

You will likely feel very pleased with your fancy watch. But all you really *needed* was the plastic watch from the bottom of your cereal box. In terms of the problem to be solved (getting to work on time), the fancy watch was a poor use of your resources (money).

When you work on projects, you may similarly find that some decisions are not in alignment with the problem to be solved.

Cameron fell victim to this when he decided to pursue a solution that aligned more closely with his hobbies than the customer's requirements. In engaging in CV-Driven Development (CDD), he neglected to consider what was important for the customer (solving their problem), and focused instead on ticking off items from his wish list to improve the attractiveness of himself as a CTO, and CamelCat Marketing as a tech company.

OPTIMISING FOR THE FUTURE

You may find that mistakes are made when attempting to predict how a solution will be used.

We do not always have the luxury of working on a project to modernise an existing system that is well-documented, battle-tested, and has long-established public contracts. Often—

especially when doing agency work—we find ourselves on greenfield projects that are a nightmare to build for precisely the same reason they are a joy to build: there are few clear rules about what is required.

Greenfield projects promise something special to developers: that finally, for once in their career, they can do things the right way, from the beginning. They can write beautiful, well-structured, maintainable, testable, observable code. They can use new technologies that will sharpen their skills and reduce their development time. They can even optimise for future scaling challenges, with asynchronous batch processing, microservice architecture, container orchestration, and so on and so forth (if these practices have fallen out of fashion by the time you are reading this, replace them with whatever is trending nowadays).

But this often causes issues. It is worth remembering that such optimisations are only of use if the problems they prematurely solve eventually rear their heads. And two things may stop that from occurring.

The first is that, when working to a tight, *real*, deadline, spending time on premature optimisations comes at the cost of getting the project across the line. If a project does not ship, those premature optimisations achieved nothing. There is value—no matter how painful it sometimes feels to admit—in building something as simply as possible, just to get it out there.

The second is that you may not have sufficient alignment on what the likely future problems even *are*.

Suppose you are building a product that, in theory, is usable by everyone in the world. Maybe *The World's Best Spell Checker*. The total addressable market for such a product numbers in the billions. So you forecast that within 24 months you will have to support half a billion users.

You scramble to ensure the product is scalable and as lean as possible—after all, at that kind of scale, every additional byte of code will add up to real numbers against your bottom line.

But by the two-year mark, the number of users has long plateaued. You have millions of users—an incredible feat by any modern standard, but nowhere near what you had predicted.

Your product has lived up to its title, and has performed very well within its niche, but it did not change the world as you anticipated. The vast majority of the premature optimisations were a waste of time, because the vision was not equal to reality.

Just as Mission Critical is the desired end state of a Stroke of Genius solution, the end state of solutions where Vision ≠ Reality (at least where the problem is not successfully iterated on) is to become a Waste of Time. Early data may have suggested that the work had to be done, but reality did not bear that out.

This can also occur when the scope of a project is not clear, or is not correctly understood. If, for example, those building the solution have inferred that it may have to support tens of thousands of users, when in reality it is being sold to a single company with no more than a few hundred employees.

BUILDING FOR THE WRONG AUDIENCE

When researching a problem, it is also possible to rely *too* heavily on the feedback and advice of individuals.

One issue is that not everyone is outgoing, well-spoken, or opinionated. You may find that those most willing to engage with you and/or provide significant insights are not representative of the primary users of the eventual solution. They may even lack the requisite context and knowledge to understand the true scope of the problem.

Ensuring that you speak to the *right* people as early as possible is therefore extremely important. You do not want to rely solely upon the feedback of those who shout the loudest.

In all but the smallest of companies, individuals are usually not responsible for choosing the specific tools they use in their jobs. It generally makes business sense for people doing the same job to use the same tools, and for someone in a position of authority to choose what those tools are. It also often makes sense for one individual (or group) to be responsible for vendor relations, putting requirements out to tender and licensing suitable tools.

In a tech-enabled company, this may be the responsibility of the IT Manager.

But this often creates an issue: that those providing a solution and those using it may never speak, or even know of each other's existence. Those doing the *buying* are often assessing solutions to problems that they themselves do not experience.

This becomes even more complicated when commissioning a bespoke solution, where several layers of management—and multiple lines of communication—might exist between the users and the builders. They will likely have a way to exchange information with each other, but it may take days or even weeks to receive a response to a relatively simple query, as the message is forwarded through each layer of management.

Worse, crucial details may be lost in the process, especially if a single stakeholder in the chain decides (usually with good intentions) to act as a filter for information. If that person is not the most knowledgeable about the problem being solved *and* the goals of the business, the end result will not be optimal.

However, in the quest to avoid siloed communication and decision-making, it is important not to just include as many people in the process as possible. Too many cooks, after all, spoil the broth. Many stakeholders who can freely converse are better than a single stakeholder, but only if they are close to the problem that is being solved.

REVISITING PAST PROJECTS

Finally, it is important to regularly revisit your assumptions about what is Mission Critical and what you believe is a Stroke of Genius.

What does the latest research and user sentiment say? Industry trends, staff turnover, and changing consumer demographics can affect both the problems being experienced, and the demand for a particular solution. It is important to ensure that what worked yesterday is still working today.

It is when problems shift and appetites change that your Mission Critical and Stroke of Genius solutions may begin to occupy the space where Vision ≠ Reality. When this happens, you have two options: innovate, or abandon.

The world does not stand still, and that is largely a good thing. If we did not strive for bigger and better solutions to age-old problems, it is not an exaggeration to say that modern society could not exist. Continuous advancements in agriculture, irrigation, transportation, sanitation, and medicine (for example) have made it possible for humans to live in enormous cities, travel the world, and spend their lives working on problems that are unrelated to day-to-day survival.

Change will always come. And if you do not figure out how to evolve your solutions—to make them once again compatible with your customers' problems—someone else will.

You also have the option of abandoning a project, rather than attempting to reinvent it. There is no shame in this, especially if you do not have the resources required to regain relevance. You just need the courage to acknowledge that you have spent significant quantities of time, money, and energy on something that is (or is soon to be) no longer fit for purpose.

This is one of the hardest decisions to make in the lifecycle of a project. But, sometimes, the best thing you can do is burn down the castle to reclaim the land.

WASTE OF TIME

SOMETIMES WE BUILD things that we shouldn't. We may jump the gun and anticipate an unvalidated demand. Or perhaps we just want to put something new and shiny on our CV.

Whatever the reason; we've ended up building something that no one asked for, and that no one is using. Such solutions are a Waste of Time.

There are opportunities to salvage a Waste of Time solution by challenging your assumptions and committing to a radical pivot.

There are also opportunities to accept that the effort to salvage a Waste of Time is too large a burden, given the available capacity and the current priorities; that the best outcome stems from cutting your losses and burning down the castle you have spent so much time erecting.

EXPLORING A STROKE OF GENIUS

A potential Stroke of Genius is a precarious thing, as, by definition, it lacks demand from the market.

User acceptance testing (UAT) will hopefully validate the idea and begin to create that demand, but in the earlier stages of development it is anyone's guess whether the solution is a veritable Stroke of Genius, or a regrettable Waste of Time. And like Schrödinger's cat, you will not know which it is until you measure it.

To minimise your risk, aim to get something into users' hands as soon as possible. First, build a minimum viable product (MVP), and collect as much data as possible. Collect quantitative data with automated tools, and qualitative data from user interviews.

If the data supports your hypothesis, use it to iteratively refine your Stroke of Genius, and deliver something that truly delights your users.

If, however, the quantitative data suggests that no one will use the solution, and the qualitative data suggests that no one identifies with the problem you are attempting to solve, it may be time to pull the plug.

Your aim should be to always remain objective. Identify your efforts as a Waste of Time as early as possible, if that is what the data is telling you. And allow yourself to do so before so much time and effort has been expended that killing it off becomes a psychological and emotional challenge.

CHASING SHINY THINGS

When we lack data to guide our efforts, we risk building things of ambiguous value because they present in a pleasing manner. *The latest and greatest technology*—whatever that is—is always appealing, as we are attracted to its novelty and the premise that it must, by definition, be better than what came before.

When we do this intentionally, we end up with CDD;

solutions built that benefit the reputation of the builder more than they benefit those experiencing the problem.

It is easy to assume that CDD is the product of selfish individuals who place their own value above that of their colleagues and their company. Although you may encounter individuals like this from time to time (Cameron certainly has his moments), you cannot always assume selfishness as the root cause.

Sometimes, such decision making stems from a desire to be good at one's job.

In the modern world, the value of your CV is immense. Your professional experiences bring reward and recognition. They directly allow you to tick off a number of items on Maslow's Hierarchy of Needs: from money to buy shelter and food, through to the belonging and esteem earned from peers when your efforts are recognised.

Ergo, something that looks good on your CV is generally good for your prospects of survival and emotional fulfilment.

Reverse engineering that logic, you can fall into the trap of assuming that the best practices and technologies can be found on the CVs of those who boast the highest levels of personal and professional success.

When we follow such 'best practices' without question, we fall victim to *cargo culting*, a phenomenon where individuals or groups mimic the behaviour of others, which they believe to be the direct cause of some tangentially related benefit.

The most well-known example comes from the aftermath of World War II. During the war, some Pacific peoples had inferred causation between military activity in the area and the simultaneous introduction of novel goods obtained from soldiers. When the soldiers withdrew and took the goods with them, cults were established to simulate the now-absent military activity, reasoning that the goods (cargo) would thereafter return.

Relating this back to technology, we often see that teams mimic the processes of successful companies, expecting success to logically follow.

However, it is usually the case that those processes are implemented *because* of the company's success, not the other way round.

Consider massive microservice architecture and container orchestration. Will running thousands of microservices in Kubernetes make a tech company as successful as the crème de la crème of Silicon Valley? Or do the top Silicon Valley tech companies *need* that kind of architecture because their technology stack would otherwise collapse under the weight of their massive success?

We saw how Cameron attempted to introduce machine learning to find success, with the premise that it could enable human-level recognition and pattern matching inside a magic black box. And there are certainly plenty of success stories to reinforce this perception; whether it is AI connecting the dots to solve a string of crimes that humans considered unrelated, or machines beating humans at *chess* and *go*.

But those success stories almost always involve massive scale and unimaginable amounts of data. The kind of scale at which Cameron and CamelCat Marketing were nowhere near to operating. Machine learning would look good on Cameron's CV, and even build up some industry hype around CamelCat Marketing. But, at their comparatively tiny scale, it was not the silver bullet they supposed.

When allowed to enter into a project unchecked, a shiny thing may become the direct cause of failure. Leaving everyone to scratch their head and ask, 'Why didn't it work? We even used the shiny thing!'

IDEALISED BUILDING

Solutions can also manifest as a Waste of Time when the reasons for building them are aligned more closely with personal goals than the problem itself.

Robert sought only to work on projects that served a greater good, and Cameron wanted to focus on things that excited him.

Some motivations can be more readily empathised with than others, and ideally we are able to cater to them all. But when we focus more on fulfilling personal desires than on solving the problems presented by paying clients, we risk disillusioning those clients and then having *no* projects to cherrypick from. This was the dilemma Dru found herself in, where she took on projects she did not love, in order to keep the lights on.

Even the most personally satisfying solution is a Waste of Time if no one asked for it, and no one uses it.

Of course, that does not excuse being complacent about building bad things. Trade-offs must often be made, and the skill is in knowing where exactly to draw the line.

CULLING AN IDEA IF IN DOUBT

You will not always have enough information to determine if something is worth working on.

Generally, an unproven solution will be built iteratively, with feedback sought early and often. But what if you are chasing a big idea, that no one has asked for, and your time, money, and people are torn between it and something else that has a solid chance of success? Are you willing (or even able) to put all your eggs in one basket for a project that *may or may not* deliver a worthwhile return on investment?

Don't shy away from being realistic about the limitations you face. Even if [without those limitations] an idea is pure gold, if you are unable to execute on it and execute on it well, it will fall squarely into the Waste of Time category.

And from there it can be abandoned.

But the brilliant thing about brilliant ideas is their resilience. If you truly have an idea worth pursuing, you won't be able to stop it from reappearing time and again on your roadmap. When the time is right and you have the means of making a success of it, it will be there waiting.

IT DOESN'T COUNT IF THE PROBLEM ISN'T SOLVED

When you think in terms of *problems to be solved* rather than *features to be built*, you begin to realise that, if your efforts don't actually solve the problem, none of your active users really count.

Consider Cameron's misguided vision. The intention was to make something that reduced human intervention. His solution would have been widely used by the target audience. But both ML-Cast and his own machine learning models were observed to behave in undesirable ways. Had either been allowed through to production, it is conceivable that *more* humans would end up in the mix, either to vet its output, or to clean up its mistakes. The problem—of reducing human intervention—would *not* have been solved.

Alice saw that the problem was not being solved, and took drastic action by removing the offending solution entirely.

DIGGING YOURSELF OUT OF A HOLE

Sometimes, opinions are conflicted over whether to attempt to salvage a failing project. Many voices may be calling for abandonment, while one—typically the one with *veto* power—

insists on moving forward, like a cartoonish prospector digging for long-exhausted gold, saying things like:

 Don't worry about the size of the hole—if we just keep digging, we'll be rich!

Think about the commonalities of failing projects (either pre- or post-launch). They miss deadlines. They go over budget. The team building them doubles or triples in size. And for each day that passes, the best-guess estimate for finishing the work slips back by two days. For those in charge, failure often does not seem like an option.

Sometimes it will pay off. The common refrain in the tech industry is, after all, *fake it 'til you make it.*

But just as common in the tech industry is the fact that the vast majority of companies neither achieve their stated goal, nor survive beyond a few years. Venture capitalists invest hundreds of millions on the understanding that their returns will come from only a small number of the companies they invest in.

The same logic can apply to projects. If you are running a portfolio of ten projects, the odds are good that one of them will be a massive success. But if you are 18 months into a three-month project and that is all you are responsible for? The odds are stacked against you.

Six months into the three-month project, it looks bad that you have spent double the allotted time. But it's only a few months, so you accept the mistake and continue. *Eighteen* months into the project, you then must continue on principle: admitting to have wasted so much time seems unforgivable. But think about what you could have done with those last twelve months, had you given up earlier. Perhaps you could have completed many smaller, *successful* projects.

It can be humiliating to admit that something we have

poured time into has not worked. Time is our only true commodity, and we have a limited supply of it. We cannot buy more of it, or trade something else for it. As humans, it is not pleasant to realise that we have wasted something so precious. Whether that time was spent on a work project, a doomed romantic relationship, or a book with an unsatisfactory ending.

So making the decision to abandon something we have poured time into is difficult. We may worry about the damage to our reputation if we bring a project to an unsuccessful close. We might even try to convince everyone (ourselves included) that, if we just keep working, eventually we will strike that gold. We may even be admired for our sheer determination.

Because the metaphorical gold will always appear to be just a few feet further down. And who knows? With enough time and effort it may even be reached. But very few projects can wait forever.

Dru accepted and tacitly endorsed the ever-spiralling Project Accelerate out of desperation, and hopes for a miracle. Only the looming loss of her business was enough to de-risk the alternative. Because, at that point, there was nothing additional to lose.

Ideally you won't wait that long.

However painful it may be, you can cut your losses early if you can learn to recognise when the carrot you are chasing is dangling from a stick attached to your own back. Your reputation may suffer, you may miss out on a promotion, and you will have to live with the loss of your precious time. But you will instantly gain capacity to explore new opportunities.

Don't be the prospector giddily hugging a lump of gold at the bottom of a pit so deep they cannot climb back out.

REALIGNING AGAINST THE ORIGINAL PROBLEM

Sometimes a solution just fails. Maybe the implementation was so poor that those who tried to use it quickly abandoned it. Maybe it was so far off the mark that no one even *attempted* to use it. Maybe the market demand was just too low.

Whatever the reason, you end up with a Waste of Time on your hands. But you can take one last stab at salvaging it.

Go back to basics. The solution may have failed terribly, but there must have been a reason to pursue it in the first place. Look beyond the implementation details—the concrete solution—and think about what prompted the project in the first place. What was the underlying problem that needed to be solved?

This was the path Alice followed when deciding to scrap the work in progress, and focus on reworking Purple Budgie Finance's existing CRM system. The project's *execution* had been bad, but not its *intent*.

It is always worth critically reassessing your understanding of how closely a solution aligns with the problem it is intended to solve, and the validity of that problem. If the problem stands up to scrutiny, trying again always remains an option.

When Alice pivoted Project Accelerate, she committed to giving up on the previous approach and removing what had been perceived as the killer feature. Although the execution had failed, the problem remained, and the positives of addressing it outweighed the negatives of not. Digging deep into the *why* of the problem helped her to arrive at a solution that solved the problem in a much more effective manner.

IMPLEMENTING THE MODEL

APPLYING PREEMPTIVELY

HOW THE MODEL is applied depends on how far you are in the development cycle. Is the solution ready for beta testing? Or is it still an idle shower thought that you haven't yet put down onto paper?

If your solution is already in users' hands, it is possible to gauge its performance retrospectively (more on that later). This is usually easy, as you will have hopefully accumulated data over time—user analytics collected, successes noticed and celebrated, fires burning and complained about, etc.

But what about the earlier stages, when you are still in the throes of planning and building?

Superficially, most solutions will easily fit into a single quadrant of the model. The well-researched, tried-and-tested linchpin of your product is Mission Critical. The wacky new idea that will disrupt the industry and crush your competitors is a Stroke of Genius. The wrong end of the stick you picked up and ran with is where Vision ≠ Reality. And the regrettable tangent you fell in love with and spent all your time and money on is the Waste of Time.

So, having those labels at your disposal, how can you act preemptively to ensure that you build the right thing, take the right chances, and course-correct before it's too late?

BUILDING THE ESSENTIAL

At the beginning of any project, focusing on the Mission Critical components is a sensible choice. And it starts with asking a relatively easy question: *What problem needs to be solved?*

It is easy to make assumptions, and to rely on others' expertise to intuitively know the answer to this question. Oscar assumed the solutioneers at CamelCat Marketing could solve his problem without articulating to anyone (even himself) what that problem actually was.

Whether you are building a single feature, a new product, or an entire business, you must be able to describe the problem to be solved. As a businessperson, your elevator pitch should be well-rehearsed. This should also be true if you are a planner or a builder. *Anyone* who is involved in the process of building something essential should be able to clearly articulate not just *what* they are building, but *why*—what problem is being solved, who the end user is, and what the positive impact will be to them.

If your people cannot describe what they are building and why, you should spend time helping them understand. Whether that involves slideshow presentations or client site visits (or something else entirely!) is up to you. But you must ensure everyone understands the goal.

But if *you* cannot convincingly describe what you are building and why, that is something else entirely. You may have to ask yourself some hard questions, such as: *Do people actually need this?* and, *Will it be at least as easy to use as the incumbent solution?* This is where the real value came from Alice's conversation with Oscar: she forced an understanding of what was to be built and why.

Be preemptive and ask these questions whenever you begin solutionising, before any serious time has been spent on building or prototyping. Be prepared for frank introspection and to be proven wrong. Humility should be table stakes for participation at this stage.

Ultimately, you should be certain you are tackling the right problems, and be able to explain your mission in simple terms. This is important because it is rare that anything is built in a silo; the work done tomorrow is usually built on top of the work done today, and mistakes compound over time. By ensuring that your proposed solution aligns with a *real* problem rather than a *perceived* one, you are setting yourself up for success down the line.

Having satisfied yourself (and hopefully others!) that the plan makes sense, it is time to involve potential customers to kick the tyres.

Now, let's talk about that word: *customers*. There is a very important distinction we need to make. It may sound bizarre, but the customer is usually not the person who buys the thing you have built; the customer is instead the person who *uses* it.

Think about it: unless you are operating solely in the B2C (Business-to-Consumer) space, your direct interaction with end users is often zero. Both at the point of creating the solution, and at the point of its use. You will instead interact with decision makers who represent them.

A decision maker may be a line manager, a vendor manager, or even a company owner. And that individual's job is to make purchasing decisions for the company's employees. In the context of a typical corporation, they are the ones who long ago decided to go all in on software from IBM, Microsoft, Google, or some other provider. They picked the e-mail provider, the office suite, and the brand of computer you use.

If you are building solutions, this is what your relationship with your customers might look like:

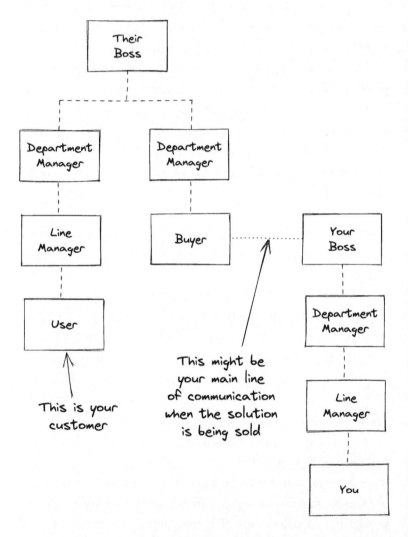

The odds are high that you have worked for a company that forced you to use a particular piece of software that was entirely wrong for the problem your job required you to solve: it was too slow, it lacked basic features, or it had just not kept up with changes in the industry. The odds are also high that, when you or a colleague once enquired about switching to another package, the answer was, 'Sorry, we only use X. Bob in Corporate's in charge of that.'

But who the hell was Bob? Whoever he was, he had obviously never done your job. You might have wondered why he made decisions that had such a negative impact on everyone's productivity. *If only he had sat with us and took the time to understand what we actually did, productivity wouldn't be so low,* you might have thought.

As a solution provider, you will often find yourself talking to Bobs. They mean well, they buy within their budget, and they generally have a good understanding of the business requirements. But it is rare for them to actively involve those they are buying on behalf of in the consultation process.

———

BOB IN THE MIDDLE

Imagine you are Bob: well-meaning, and intent on doing your job (replacing an outdated piece of clerical software) without bothering those who are busy doing the actual work.

You find a vendor and, after a lengthy period of development, roll the new solution out to users. You have been testing every beta release that comes your way, and it looks great, so you wait for the stamp of approval from the users.

You hear crickets.

You enquire why, and discover that their department's IT budget is smaller than yours; their computer monitors have a low resolution, and several of the application's most important CTAs are off-screen.

But the software will solve many problems, so you're sure you'll get some more development budget to fix it.

You borrow some larger monitors from another department so testing can resume. But you discover a new blocker.

The solution's killer feature (a significantly faster record search) has an issue. It turns out that it also requires a billing code, to increase performance by first narrowing the field of search to records for a single project. But billing codes are complex, and only obtainable by first searching for the record(s) to which they are attached.

Back to the drawing board with that feature.

But the software will solve many problems, so you're sure you'll get some more development budget to fix it.

Right?

————

If Bob doesn't expose you to the end users—your real customers —you need to be proactive in the matter. How exactly you do that is a problem for you to solve. Politics may make it difficult to get in a room with them, but the effort is worth it.

Some end users will be articulate and well-informed of the

problems they face. They may even have ideas or prior experiences to draw on, and suggestions to make to you. You don't have to build exactly what they tell you, of course, but if you speak to enough users you are likely to hear the same core messages over and over. Those universal problems are the ones to focus on.

But some end users are not aware of what their problems really are. Oscar filled the role of both the buyer *and* the end user who hadn't thought hard enough about the nature of their problems. With such individuals you will need to be patient, and ask questions to understand why they do what they do. If you can pull this off, patterns will once more emerge that your objective eye will pick up on.

Perhaps they engage in lengthy manual processes that have become a recurring part of their job. Consider what could you automate to eliminate unnecessary time and effort. Especially the time and effort that no one bothers to question, simply because it has been that way for so long and is just the cost of doing business.

Then on to building.

If the obvious thing(s) to build do not already exist and you're not in a race to market against your competitors—that is, if you've truly got a unique approach to solving an old problem —it is advisable to stop for a moment and look to the past. You want to avoid tripping up on hidden obstacles.

Look hard. Who—if anyone—had previously tried to build something similar? If you find someone, for what reasons did they fail?

Spend time understanding their approach and how the market reacted. If the demand from end users for such a solution has existed for 20 years, but for 19 of those years the technology required to pull it off didn't exist, you need to understand in detail what has changed in the last year, and be confident that you really are now unblocked and stand a chance of succeeding where others failed.

But remember that, with Mission Critical solutions, you are normally not trying to change the world—your level of innovation likely tops out at finding a better and / or quicker way to solve a problem for which a worse-performing solution already exists. You are not attempting to reinvent the wheel, just to build it, and maybe grease the axles a little.

Alice achieved this by realising that existing components— the CRM, automated customer e-mails, and reminders for Purple Budgie Finance's staff to carry out manual actions—could be daisy-chained together to solve their core problems in a novel and more efficient way.

———

WHEN A DIRECT LINK ISN'T EASY ENOUGH

If you built a web-based system that was, essentially, a state machine, you may send automated e-mails to stakeholders to keep things flowing whenever it is their turn to get involved.

But online systems require passwords, and passwords are often inconvenient and difficult to remember. You might find that e-mails go out, but some users do not bother logging in. Projects grind to a halt.

Can you simplify the Mission Critical, two-stage process of *Click Link* and *Log In*?

What if the e-mail links contained short-lived authentication codes (often called *magic links*)? Authentication would still take place, but the effort required from users would be significantly reduced.

———

So once you know *what* to build, the task becomes building it as efficiently as possible: if you have built something similar before, take cues from what did and did not work during that project; if you have existing infrastructure and pipelines, take advantage of them so you have one less thing to build; etc. Your Mission Critical functionality should be so well-defined at this point that is it difficult to get carried away and overcomplicate it.

But don't follow the past blindly. At the start of a new project, take a moment to critically assess the prior experiences and knowledge you intend to rely on, *just in case* something has changed. Is your experience from 10 years ago still valid, or have subtle nuances emerged in the way the industry solves the various small problems that come together to solve your larger Mission Critical problem?

Above all else, speak at length—and often—to your end users (your customers!), feel their pain, and build what they *need*.

TAKING A CHANCE

Every so often, you get the chance to shake things up and delight your customers. Maybe you disrupt the industry and make your competitors appear slow and dated. Maybe—just maybe—you get to change the world.

Regardless of the scale of your efforts, the right factors need to coincide: you need a genius idea; there needs to be an appetite for change; and the infrastructure to support your radical new offering must exist *and* be affordable. Making a Stroke of Genius solution successful is as much the result of luck and timing as anything else.

With so much of the equation out of your hands, it becomes doubly important to nail the parts of the creative process that *are* within your control.

Your quest is to create something novel that no one realised they needed. So start by considering the status quo.

Humans will put up with a lot of inconvenience if the net result is positive. Most processes contain inefficient steps. And because the end result is acceptable, these steps will often go unquestioned. Maybe they even form part of a superstition or received wisdom. Does chicken soup really help you get over a cold, or do you just resort to it when you're feeling your worst, right before the symptoms begin to subside?

Your customers will have their own chicken soups. Find out what they take for granted that has not been critically assessed. Ask the question, *Could there be a better way?* Or better yet, *Is this even the best outcome?* What could you change or invent to radically increase the net benefit?

What if, instead of chicken soup, you came up with some concoction that demonstrably halved the average recovery time, replacing the placebo with an actual cure? Think on the wider implications of that for a moment. The effect on the economy and human wellbeing would be huge, with output, productivity, and happiness increased across the board as people feel well more often.

So how can you find those inefficiencies and improve upon them?

As with Mission Critical planning, speak to the people doing the work. If possible, observe them while they work. As an impartial outsider, many inefficiencies will jump out at you. You may not see the solution yet, but the rabbit holes will present themselves—typically in the areas you find yourself wondering, 'Why on earth are they doing *that*?!'

————

NEW SOLUTIONS TO OLD PROBLEMS

E-commerce was a huge, emerging industry in the early 2000s. But as brick-and-mortar stores pivoted into online sales, the technology to support them was still in its infancy.

Much of the work of selling online, ironically, ended up being clerical and manual in nature. An average morning for an e-commerce employee might involve hours spent manually franking packing slips for the day's orders.

But what if, instead of printing, franking, and folding those packing slips by hand, a small piece of software had been introduced to download details of the day's orders, notify the courier of the parcel details via their web service, and print pre-franked, sticky packing labels en masse from a thermal printer?

————

Sounds easy, right? Rock up, watch people work, tell them how they're doing it all wrong, save the day.

Except... that will not make you popular. Don't underestimate how easy it is to shoot yourself in the foot.

If your sales pitch essentially boils down to telling people they've been doing everything wrong, it doesn't matter how game-changing your new solution is. People spend a large percentage of their lives at work—almost half of their waking hours in an average week. That is a huge chunk of their lives. For you to then suggest it was all a waste? People will have feelings about that. If your new solution is game-changing enough, they may even start to worry about their job security.

This, fundamentally, is perhaps the most significant challenge you will face. And from which direction(s) this challenge will come can be unpredictable. It may be end users, middle management, the C-suite, or anyone in-between. There is no quicker way to create discontent among people than to change something (anything, in fact). When our jobs keep a roof over our heads and food on our tables, any sign of change triggers a primal worry.

So it is on you to create the conditions where the benefit can become apparent. This is the challenge every startup founder faces, and is the challenge you will face any time you try to innovate something new.

As previously suggested, having an open line of communication with those whose problems you are attempting to solve is important. Being able to observe them is ideal. Get in the room if you can.

Seek their feedback, but focus on their frustrations. They may not tell you what to build, but you should be able to see where opportunities exist, and you can ask questions to validate your thinking. This is how Julie's *condolence package* idea came about.

But don't get overly technical—they probably don't speak the managementese or know the industry jargon and acronyms you're used to sharing with the company's representatives. They're just humans, trying to do a job, probably with a less-than-ideal set of tools at their disposal. Plain, simple language is enough to explore the baffling norms they put up with.

If you are an industry outsider, even better. Your lack of context will make coming up with radical new ways of working easier; there will be no received wisdom to trample your ideas with pesky *well, actually…* discourse.

If end users are not available (or if the target market does not yet exist), it can be useful to test the solution internally. This is something you should be doing anyway, in the form of alpha testing, and it can be increased in scope if there is no alternative source of users. When it comes alpha testing, try to get your back-office staff involved: those folk who have the least direct involvement with product development.

At some point, you will need to convince someone (perhaps not end users) to buy the solution. Or, if it is an enhancement to what they are already using, to *buy into* its use. The extent to which your vision is radically different will dictate how difficult it will be to get that buy-in. After all, novelty carries with it risk, and in business, *risk = money*. Your job in the earliest stages is to expose others to the vision, and in the later stages to get them to agree to its implementation.

Do a demo, run a free trial alongside the existing solution… whatever derisks the upgrade enough that you can showcase the various benefits. This could involve giving your clients side-by-side access to an upgraded system, or it could mean a nationwide advertising campaign asking the public to reconsider a small part of how they live their lives. And everything in between. It really depends on the scope of your Stroke of Genius.

However you do it, your goal should be to shatter the assumption that there is not a better way. You need to make any other approach seem backward. This is what will eventually turn your Stroke of Genius into a veritable piece of Mission Critical functionality.

But above all else, you need to ensure that what you are building can actually make it to market. If luck and ability are not on your side, or the timing is wrong, the appetite for your solution (or its ability to even deliver on the promise) will be missing and your Stroke of Genius will instead become a veritable Waste of Time. This was arguably the case with CamelCat Marketing's intended use of machine learning: established, generalised models capable of working accurately with tiny datasets were not available, and all efforts to build one were beyond the ability of the team.

If your vision is strong, and you have the will and means to pursue it long-term, you may at this point decide to pivot to something more palatable and likely to be adopted by the market in which you find yourself. It will take time, but you can then lay the groundwork for your magnum opus with each iterative release, having a significant lead on your competitors when the market conditions are finally right.

But if you don't have the means to play the long game? You have to decide whether to bet on your grand vision and hope that luck and timing converge on you while you still have working capital—whatever form that takes. This is what Cameron decided, when parting ways with CamelCat Marketing to set up his own machine learning business.

Do your homework, and ensure that your vision really is novel. It may save you a lot of time, effort, money, and disappointment. If your research shows that others have failed where you intend to succeed, make sure you have good, realistic grounds for optimism this time round. Depending on the size of the bet, it may be your only one.

GETTING BACK ON TRACK

Planning for the top two quadrants of the model is straightforward: you are building things people will use. That is the whole point of building something, after all—planning Mission Critical and Stroke of Genius work is really just *planning*.

Dealing preemptively with the bottom two quadrants of the model is an exercise in recognising as early as possible that the predicted level of use is failing to materialise, acting quickly to understand why, and taking steps to rectify the situation.

Let's consider what can be done when Vision ≠ Reality—when your alpha and beta tests clearly show that you have misunderstood the users' requirements, or that they have put too much faith in a silver-bullet solution to a much deeper-rooted problem.

It is a tough situation to find yourself in. You may have dedicated a significant amount of time and effort to get this far. So you must be brave.

Don't bury your head in the sand and continue as though nothing is wrong. Hard work does not automatically result in success. Especially if you are responsible for only a small part of the project. The option to reassess is always on the table.

Some business leaders will boast that, 'When a client says, "Jump," we only ask, "How high?"' This is a trait shared by Cameron. It generally comes from a good place—aiming to delight clients by not questioning their requirements—but it typically leads to disaster when those requirements do not pan out.

When faced with an impending disaster, you may tell yourself that, by hunkering down, and following the plan to the letter, everything will work out in the end. Or maybe you'll consider that, when the inevitable disaster *does* occur, it will at least be someone else's fault. Sales got the message wrong. The account managers and business analysts went off down the wrong rabbit holes. Everyone except you is bad at their job.

It's a compelling narrative. But don't get sucked into it.

So you must become vulnerable. You must admit that you have been building something that is missing the mark, and you need those who can make tough decisions about the project to share in that vulnerability. You may need to go back to the drawing board, which is not easily done if there are many other stakeholders.

The people involved are important. The difference between a Mission Critical solution and where Vision ≠ Reality could be as small as which group of people kicked off the project: those buying, or those who will be using. Ask who else might have been overlooked in those earlier stages—can their needs and/or insight now be examined?

However you can, break down silos and open lines of communication. Have a back-to-basics discussion, like the one Alice initiated with Oscar. Expose everyone to the big picture. Prepare for awkward moments of introspection where the failures are all laid bare.

Then learn from them.

Get the group to critically reassess not only the proposed solution, but also the original problem. Do not be afraid of asking for clarity when something is unclear. In fact, to avoid the risk of biasing the discovery process, your main question to stakeholders should be one of clarification: 'Why is that?' This is how Alice got to the root cause of the problem her colleagues were attempting to solve.

Listen to all the complaints, frustrations, and suggestions. Get people to use the solution and observe in horror as they repeatedly click the wrong button. Compare and contrast the solution's intention with the stark reality before you. Get close to the heart of why the solution is just not hitting the mark.

Then turn your embarrassment and frustration into exciting plans.

You built something that missed the mark, and that is disappointing. But by gathering insights, you can learn where you went wrong. And from those insights you can form a plan to get back on track.

It is important throughout this process to remain objective. Without bias or preconception, try to really understand the difference between what your users *want* and what they *need*. It is easy to confuse the two. Aim to fall out of love with the original solution, but do not rush to fall in love with a new one. The feedback you gather needs to be scrutinised objectively; it really must solve the problem your customers are experiencing.

Consider going back to basics and focusing on core functionality before thinking about bells and whistles. Often, a simple, effective solution is all that is required. But if bells and whistles are an important part of the plan, make sure they are backed up by data. This is where A/B testing can be invaluable.

Again, observe your customers' behaviour. If they consistently click five buttons in order to perform one task, and *only* to perform that one task, it is a no-brainer to simplify that particular user journey into a single click. But be careful! If you don't have data to back that hypothesis up, you may end up removing buttons that are used for other flows, and unintentionally decimate your customers' productivity.

OPTIMISING FOR AN IDEAL WORLD

Fast forward a few years in the world of e-commerce. Software now exists to automate much of the clerical work, but it is not standardised—many online retailers roll their own e-commerce solutions.

Among other things, these solutions must be able to retrieve orders, print packing labels, and mark those orders as *dispatched*. Maybe some bells and whistles exist (e.g.

automated e-mails to the customer), but the core functionality does two things:

1) Ensures orders are shipped;
2) Ensures orders are shipped only once.

Profit margins, and all that.

A developer working on such a system might hatch a plan to combine the various steps of that dispatch flow, replacing them with a single button that sequentially executes every step, to ensure no order is accidentally processed more than once.

But in production, sometimes the printer runs out of ink, a packing slip is lost, or faulty goods are returned and replacements need to be sent. And it is now impossible to retrigger the individual steps.

Oops.

———

After introspection and planning, you must ask a tough question: *Is the rework worth it?*

You must assess the difficulty, effort, time, and money required to get the solution back on track. You must also consider other commitments that could complicate matters, such as new projects, staffing limitations, and the difficulty and knock-on effects of securing the necessary budget.

Seriously consider whether it is better for all involved to abandon the project and cut their losses. It is not a decision to be taken lightly, but there is no shame in burning down the castle.

Assuming you make the decision to proceed and attempt to fix things, you will need to make a lot of sensible (read: boring) choices. Curtailing extraneous work will become a large part of your job. Understand (and convince others) that there will be time for optimisations and embellishments later, after you have actually shipped a usable solution.

Throughout everything, always try to be brave.

Make tough decisions. Pivot away from something you love that does not help your customer solve their problem— remember that it is for their benefit, not yours. Throw away solutions that are too far gone. And embrace the *maintenance* phase as you monitor, observe, and learn how your solution is being used in the real world.

Rinse. Repeat.

BURNING DOWN THE CASTLE

Sometimes, you just need to down tools and call it a day.

When you come up with a genius idea, or go all in on a hunch, you are taking a risk if you have not done your homework. The thing you built that no one asked for, but which you are sure will change everything, is only as good as its level of adoption. Will that anticipated use come? Quite often, a coin toss yields more favourable results.

When the market's reaction is a resounding *no thank you*, you can be sure that your solution has been a Waste of Time.

We have already explored how to set yourself up for success with a Stroke of Genius. And so, just as the path from Vision ≠ Reality to Mission Critical is largely to retrace your steps, abandon your ego, and critically assess your assumptions, so too is the path to turn a Waste of Time solution into something that maybe—just maybe—can become a Stroke of Genius.

We won't revisit that topic. The message is largely the same: do your homework, observe users, and figure out what to build.

Let's look instead at the decision to tear things down.

There is a genuine skill in realising that it may serve the greater good to tear something down and write off large chunks of time and effort.

The scope varies: maybe it means giving up on an entire project, maybe just ripping out a single solution that fell flat on its face.

Coming to this realisation can be hard. It impacts our ego, and the sunk-cost fallacy is in full effect. Even worse is when you have to convince someone else that it's time to pull the plug or that their way of doing things has not worked out. This can put people on the defensive, with disastrous results. Cameron threw Robert under the bus, and Oscar threatened much the same to Dru. Team morale is never the same after a scapegoat is made of one of its members.

So establishing a blameless culture, and checking in early and often on progress, is essential. It should not be a complete surprise when the point comes that you realise you are *not* just a few tweaks away from having something workable, or perhaps that the market is not ready and you are simply too early to the party, or maybe even that your idea was just plain awful.

Learning *when* to pull the plug is the crux of the skill. As a general rule, it is never too late to burn down the castle and start again. Because when you burn down the castle, you not only clear the land for something new, you wipe away all the shoddy masonry that was going to give way one day and kill a bunch of people.

But you don't want to wait too long. At CamelCat Marketing, the decision was almost left too late. Even Alice, who is arguably the parable's hero, waited for complete disaster before stepping up and suggesting that maybe it was time to think differently.

When you are building something (especially something experimental that can fail as easily as it succeeds), you should know exactly how to measure its success. Focus on measuring outputs that offer a meaningful insight. *X% of users who engaged with the solution end up interacting with Feature Y, an indication that Problem Z was solved* is far more telling than *X% of users engaged with the solution.* Although superficially similar, one metric tells you how many people *tried* to use the solution, the other tells you how many *succeeded* by using it.

Try to measure success as early as possible. As before, alpha and beta testing can make all the difference. If the numbers do not look good, you have the opportunity to conduct additional research, reassess your assumptions, and reorient your development efforts. And if the evidence is overwhelmingly negative and damning of the original premise—if salvation is more effort than rebuilding from scratch—*just kill it.*

This is, of course, easier said than done. When we believe we are on the cusp of changing everything, we form an emotional attachment to our work. But no one will thank you for soldiering on with a lost cause. Not your boss, the board of directors, the company's investors, your colleagues stuck with you on the sinking ship, and definitely not your mental health.

––––––

TO KILL, OR NOT TO KILL?

Projects can become a Waste of Time for many reasons. Sometimes they serve an overly optimistic grand plan. Sometimes they fill a desire to add cool stuff to the team's CVs. Sometimes they are just 'small' projects that end up getting away from everyone. The list goes on.

There are two scenarios that tend, more often than not, to occur with such projects.

In one scenario, after many months of soul-crushing work on a project that is objectively not fit for purpose (and still several months away from completion), someone is brave enough to pull the plug. Everyone is disappointed, a few people may even leave the team. But everyone is able to move onto the next thing, and learn from the experience.

In the other scenario, after many months of soul-crushing work on a project that is objectively not fit for purpose (and still several months away from completion), someone doubles down, hires extra people, lowers standards, and goes all in on the project. The work is eventually completed, but comes in several times over budget, and not functioning as intended. Everyone is disappointed. Everyone leaves (maybe not immediately, but sooner than they would have otherwise). The same thing happens with the next project.

———

As much as it hurts to down tools on a failed experiment, you can at least take the opportunity to breathe a sigh of relief. *It is over.*

How you proceed as you consign a piece of work to the trash is important, especially if you are in a position of authority or leadership. People will be acutely aware of the time they have just wasted. You can't give that time back to them, but they will want to know what is next, and will *need* to know what is next if you wish them to be energised enough to attempt something else—maybe a simplified solution, or just the next scheduled project. Dru looked back, leading with a contagious helplessness; Alice looked forward, leading with a vision of opportunity.

Of course, sometimes it's not obvious when the time is right to kill something off. The data may not be conclusive, or there may not be enough time to gather sufficient data. In such circumstances, you have to make a difficult decision about whether or not to persevere.

But do not fret—truly good ideas will keep coming back, no matter how often you remove them from the product backlog.

Now let's turn our attention to building on an established product that customers are already using.

Let's suppose your team utilises micro front ends. And let's also suppose, as sometimes happens, that the members of your team don't really talk to each other. Someone decides to add a big, bold CTA to move the user along the happy path of the new user journey they are building. The component is tested in isolation and looks great—it catches the eye and is easy to understand. But when integrated into the rest of the front-end application, it conflicts with a similar, pre-existing CTA elsewhere on the screen. In production, 50% of users end up clicking the wrong button.

There is now a threat to production. Maybe the other CTA relates to account signups. The company's bottom line could be impacted very quickly. In such circumstances, you should not be afraid to quickly and unapologetically rip out the new functionality, and not reintroduce it until the usability issue has been resolved. This often just means bringing people together to discuss the issue. Never underestimate the power of open communication.

Always consider the value users get from the existing system, and how it may be impacted by new work. A banner promoting a 50%-off sale is not only useless, but actively destructive, if it covers the app's *Buy* button. As was Cameron's nice, secure

OAuth flow when lack of adequate testing allowed it to break the production system.

You should also consider when and where to dedicate and direct your efforts.

Individuals, teams, and companies only have so much capital. This capital comes in the form of money, time, effort, and trust. All are finite resources, and we must ensure we strike the right balance when deciding how to deploy them. If we have the option to quickly build something that brings in money, we should probably build it. But if it takes longer to build than the company has money to stay afloat, it is not worth even considering. By abandoning it, we make way for some other option that the available capital can support.

The single-pane-of-glass feature that Evelyn showcased to Oscar (which ultimately failed to load) was a nice idea that *could* have become a Stroke of Genius. But we will never know, because it was extraneous to the problem statement and was ultimately ditched, having already consumed unnecessary time and effort that could have been better spent building the functionality that would solve the client's problem and save the company.

But do not despair: a genius idea can always be revisited. *Now or never* is rarely a condition of building something new. Giving yourself the best chance of long-term success is the name of the game.

The need to abandon something can also come out of the blue. If circumstances change, you should be receptive to drastic action. If a well-funded, well-known competitor emerges with a competing solution, you will have to do the math on whether continuing to build your solution is worth it. If you continue, you may have to compete on a much larger battlefield than you originally anticipated, whereas if you abandon, you can at least refocus your efforts elsewhere.

This is also applicable to existing solutions that are in maintenance mode. If a startup comes along that disrupts your entire industry and is eating away at your market share, you will have a similar decision to make: reinvent yourself to truly compete, or recognise that your time has passed.

You may even find that those seeking to disrupt your place in the market do not yet compete on equal footing. As *convenience* becomes increasingly important to consumers, alternative solutions that are subpar in terms of functionality can easily gain favour because of a closer alignment between brand and personal values. Just consider the rise of challenger banks in the UK in the 2010s—with only a superior app UX reflecting the value of *banking should be easy*, they gained millions of customers despite not having other Mission Critical features like support for direct debits, or in some cases even holding a banking licence. (Though important to note is that they had to close those Mission Critical gaps very quickly to fully convert and retain those users.)

And this can go both ways: customers can not only choose to go to a competitor because they identify more closely with their values, but they can choose to leave you because of a misalignment with *your* values. Values can, in fact, be a Mission Critical piece of the puzzle. This is why Robert decided to part ways with CamelCat Marketing, and why Dru was concerned about the public perception of their partnership with Owliphant Insights.

Finally (and to loop back to the beginning), if you are considering abandoning something, take the time to first reexamine the problem. Is there is a way to pivot into something else that may be successful? It is always worth considering. But if not? Burn down the castle and bask in the flames.

CHECKLISTS FOR APPLYING PREEMPTIVELY

THEY SAY that you need to hear something three times before it *really* sinks in. When exploring the model, we looked at each of the four quadrants, with some [hopefully relatable] examples of how each type of scenario could arise. Then we looked at how to apply the lessons from the model preemptively, forming ideas for actions that can be carried out in support of each quadrant of the model. Now we will distil those actions down further into checklists to focus on the key takeaways.

Referring to these checklists will make the *planning* stages of a solution more likely to yield a successful execution, and may save you from frustration further down the line.

MISSION CRITICAL

❏ Build the things that your users, clients, or customers actually require to achieve their goals

❏ Dig deep to understand the problem you are really trying to solve, getting face time with those feeling the pain of not having an efficient solution

❏ Look to the past for prior art, and consider whether the way you have previously done things can make things easier this time

❏ Don't take received wisdom for granted; verify its utility for yourself, and look to the past for examples to support or reject its candidacy for continued use

❏ Be receptive to expanding your understanding of the effectiveness of long-established ways of doing things, and embrace new best-in-class approaches that yield better results

STROKE OF GENIUS

❏ Be aware of the pain points that people accept as a standard part of the status quo, and innovate solutions to remove or improve them

❏ Understand the effort required to introduce a new idea or way of doing things—in particular how human emotion may lead to high levels of resistance—and constantly assess your ability and appetite to take on such a challenge

❏ Communicate with those whose problems you are solving early, often, and on an ongoing basis, being careful to not make assumptions about industry-specific terminology

❏ Wherever possible, use the things you are building yourself, to put yourself in the shoes of your target audience when they are not available to give you direct feedback

❏ If your big, visionary idea is something that will take a significant amount of time to gain widespread adoption, ensure that it is something you are constantly building towards, pivoting products that consumers are not yet ready for into something that they need today, whilst keeping just enough of the original idea intact to facilitate the gradual change of opinions and sentiment

❏ Make sure your genius idea really is novel, rather than something that is so unrealistic that numerous prior attempts have all failed to gain traction

VISION ≠ REALITY

❏ Resist the temptation to work to strict plans in silos to maintain your personal feeling of safety, and instead encourage cross-functional work that invites flexibility and accepts lower levels of certainty

❏ Get the right people in the room, empower each and every one of them to talk, and listen to them

❏ Don't get carried away with spending time and money on wish list solutions if that is not specifically your business—core functionality is all that is needed most of the time

❏ Be realistic about the scope of a project and how much work you need to do up front to save time down the line; there is usually a very fine balance between sensible steps to avoid common traps, and premature optimisation that never has the chance to pay off

❏ Be brave and either pivot or abandon the things that are not working out, whether they were once core functionality, or simply bets you decided to run with that you are now reassessing

WASTE OF TIME

❏ Remember that pulling the plug on experiments that failed to deliver acceptable results before you become too emotionally attached to them can be a *good* thing

❏ Don't worry about abandoning ideas if you don't have enough data to support them; a good idea will keep coming back to you

❏ Carefully consider the side effects of changes you make, and reverse them if they end up doing more harm than good

❏ Ensure that *how* you are building something benefits those who will be using it, not just yourself, and actively avoid approaches that help you but harm the effectiveness of the solution

❏ Be aware of your limitations when chasing a goal; if you expend all of your time, energy, or money on reaching it, you may miss out on other opportunities that yield better results

❏ When faced with something that does not particularly solve a problem, revisit the original motivation for building it, and investigate whether the problem still exists, and whether the solution can be pivoted to better address it

APPLYING RETROSPECTIVELY

WHEN YOUR SOLUTION is finished and has been in users' hands for some time, the model can be applied retrospectively to measure how well it aligns with expectations.

Here, we will explore a few different ways to do this.

VALIDATING PROOF OF CONCEPTS

Sometimes, when you have built a proof of concept, someone will slap a price sticker on it, sell it to clients, and immediately declare the project a roaring success. This is a difficult situation to come back from. After all, would *you* sign off on additional time and money to rebuild something that is already out there, apparently doing the job?

Maybe one day you'll get to revisit the proof of concept and build it out properly. Say, if the right people get fired or hired. But maybe you won't, and you are stuck maintaining whatever monstrosity has been forced into production. Your first task becomes ascertaining how well it is performing.

Remember the questions asked by the model.

Whether the solution is being used should be easy to measure. If you are not already, start collecting logs to provide a quick answer.

If the answer is positive, that is a good sign. Your task then turns into shoring up the guts of the proof of concept to make it more resilient.

If the answer is negative, you have likely still learnt something useful. You might have discovered that no one has used the solution. Or perhaps that they have, but it did not solve their problem. With cold, hard figures at your disposal, you can make a case for revisiting the proof of concept to address its flaws, this time mindful that it is destined for production.

EVALUATING YOUR EXECUTION

Sometimes, you—or your users—will rush to a solution, only to discover too late that it is not being used. When this happens, and you find yourself scrambling for answers, there are some contributing factors you can consider.

One factor is whether your understanding of the problem was valid. This is where Vision ≠ Reality, and is perhaps the most common cause of project failure. The crux of it is that you accidentally solved the wrong problem.

Put your ego and professional pride aside, and critically assess the solution's original aims. With the benefit of hindsight, ask whether the original idea still makes sense. Be honest and humble if it turns out you got the wrong end of the stick and ran with it. Then ask the tough question: Do the benefits of going back to the drawing board outweigh the time and effort required to do so?

Another factor to consider is whether the problem *was* correctly understood, but that the implementation fell short of actually being a viable solution.

Apply similar logic and look inward at your assumptions and planning processes. Did subject matter experts advise you? Was the solution beta tested at any point? How often and in what manner was feedback solicited during testing? Were the *right* people involved in testing?

Possibly, neither of these factors were at play, but the solution was still not used. Look closely at what has been built, and focus on the UX. If the solution solves the right problem, and really *does* solve it, is it obvious how to use it?

It can be disheartening to learn that something you painstakingly created is confusing and difficult to work with. But that is something you have the power to address.

Start by watching what the users do. If you can, physically shadow them while they work. If not, employ logging and analytics tools to understand how they interact with the solution. Aim to learn how close they come to solving their problem. Do they get 90% of the way before giving up, or do they flounder at the first hurdle?

This should feel familiar. It is similar to the process of *preemptively* learning what to build: watch users, understand where they struggle, then innovate a better way of solving their problems. You may have to undertake a radical overhaul of the solution, or you may just have to increase the size of one button. But at least you will know.

BENCHMARKING AN ENTIRE PRODUCT

You can also use the model to look back and benchmark all of a product's features. (In this section we will use the term *feature* instead of *solution*, as we are explicitly talking about features within a product.)

Start with an empty grid, ideally on a shared whiteboard, and invite those close to the product to join you in plotting its features.

Treat the axes of the grid as sliding scales. If there was more demand for Feature A than for Feature B, it should be placed further along the X axis, closer to the Mission Critical and Vision ≠ Reality quadrants than the Stroke of Genius and Waste of Time quadrants.

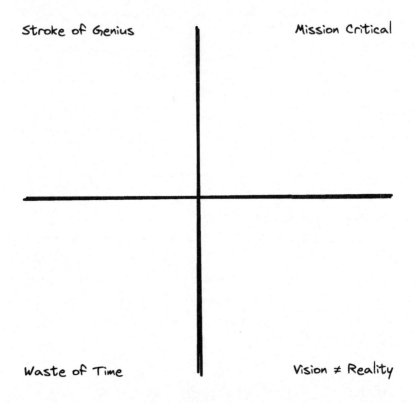

invite those close to the product to join you in plotting its

Stroke of Genius · Mission Critical · Waste of Time · Vision ≠ Reality

Try to include as many relevant stakeholders from the project as possible. Include those who built it, those who coordinated it, those who sold it, those who bought it, and those who use it. Getting these people together is important, as it will help you accurately assess the true demand for, and utilisation of, each feature.

When plotting features on the grid, be as dispassionate as possible. It is important to stick to what the data tells you. If you feel strongly that a feature should be placed elsewhere, do not worry; once you have a clear view of how the product is performing, you can figure out what changes are required to shift a feature closer to where you believe it should be.

The following diagram is an example of how features might be plotted on the grid:

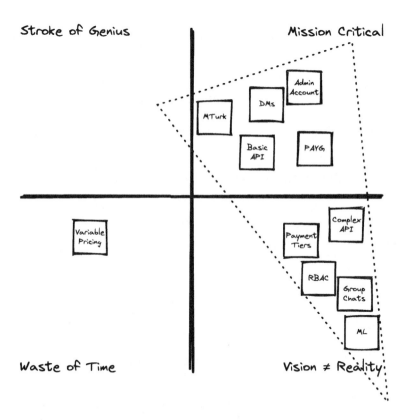

Having plotted your product's features, you can then find patterns using the incredible pattern-matching computer that is your brain.

In the example above, some features are in the Mission

Critical quadrant, an equal amount are in the Vision ≠ Reality quadrant, and one is seemingly a Waste of Time.

You may have noticed a pattern: that lesser-used features were originally deemed to be slightly more important than those that *did* see use; as illustrated by the triangle, they skew further to the right on the *users asked for it* axis.

A number of factors could be responsible: buyer's remorse; overconfidence in the ability to deliver fast, cheap, *and* well; belief in a silver-bullet solution; perhaps something else entirely. It is up to you to figure it out.

Another thing you may have noticed is that most of the features not in use are more complex versions of features that *are* in use. Direct messages versus group chats, for example. Or simple admin accounts versus complex role-based access control (RBAC) systems. This tells us something about how well the complex features were built, or how much complexity users are willing to endure to solve a given problem.

Try also to compare the features. Do high-demand/high-usage features share something in common that high-demand/low-usage features do not?

FINDING BOTTLENECKS

Finally, you can use the model to inspect the efficacy of a product's flows and user journeys.

As before, plot the product's features on the grid. Then draw lines to connect the features that together comprise a user journey. Keep it high level, and only make connections between features that are hard requirements of the user journey.

Look for bottlenecks. Do any exist that may cause users to drop off?

Consider the following example, which illustrates an online checkout flow. In short, it collects information about the user and their payment method, then delivers the content they have purchased in some novel, game-changing way.

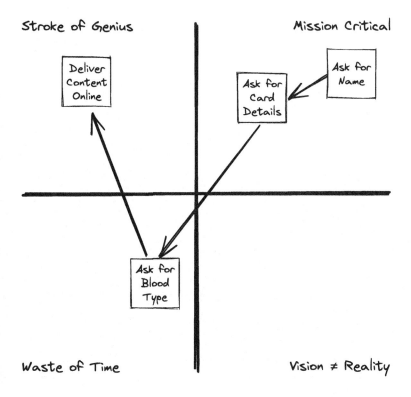

For illustrative purposes, it is an extreme example, but hopefully it is obvious why most users would drop off: online checkouts typically do not require users to provide medical details.

The first two steps are Mission Critical—it is essential to collect that information to process any online order. Data (and common sense) should show that very few users drop off here. But the third step is out of place. Perhaps, in order to save time, the checkout flow was copied from a system built for a different client where the extra information was essential. Whatever the reason, many users will abandon the flow at this point.

And so, the potential Stroke of Genius at the end of the user journey becomes a Waste of Time, because the *preceding* feature (itself a Waste of Time) prevents anyone from progressing further.

When plotting user journeys in this way, it becomes simpler to understand and address bottlenecks.

Start by asking a few questions: If you simply removed the offending step(s), would the problem immediately be resolved? Or, if doing so incurs a cost, is that cost less than the cost of doing nothing? Or, if the steps are truly essential, have you at least gained some insight into how you might rework them?

When answering these questions, follow Alice's lead and dig deep into the underlying problem. Ask *why* a lot. Identify root causes wherever they exist, to understand what is truly essential. And then make decisions to get your user journeys back on track.

Alternatively, you may discover that there is a fundamental problem with the user journey; that your and your users' requirements are at odds. Remember that you can always burn down the castle. Your killer feature is not a killer feature if no one will use it.

FINAL THOUGHTS

HOW THE MODEL FITS IN

THE MODEL primarily exists to support the development processes you likely already have in place. Namely, that you should always be learning and iterating; a central theme in most modern project and product management frameworks.

The model can be used in conjunction with others. For example, when plotting solutions onto the model's grid, it may be helpful to consider *effort* versus *reward*, using other models such as Intercom's RICE framework—if the appetite for spending time or money on a problem increases or decreases, the position of a solution on the grid may likewise change.

The model might not disrupt how you carry out most of your actual work, but it *should* help you to probe and ask the right questions about what you are building, forcing you to question how well you understand your users' needs.

Labelling a solution according to the model helps you to understand your biases surrounding the thing you are building, in the same way that you may feel relief or disappointment at the outcome of an important coin toss intended to save you from making a tough decision.

THE JOB VERSUS THE SOLUTION

ONE OF THE most important things to remember is that the concrete implementation you come up with (that is, the delivered solution) is not automatically a solution to the underlying problem. Where this is forgotten, complacency can take root and it becomes easy to blame everyone except yourself for the shortcomings in what you have built.

Always measure against a job; a description of the desired end state; a problem to be solved. In focusing first on the solution—machine learning—Cameron and Oscar were working backwards, hoping that their approach would solve the problem, rather than choosing an approach based on its ability to solve the problem. The job they should have kept in mind was *identifying cross-selling opportunities at scale*.

This is why, when Alice drilled down to understand the problem, how it was currently being solved and what the bottlenecks were, she was able to work forwards from the job. Once she had started that process, it was easy to identify that the first steps of solving the problem (collating all the relevant data) was already solved for in the form of a CRM system that otherwise performed quite well. That provided something to build on, to accelerate to a solution with the smallest levels of effort and complexity.

Bear this in mind when plotting solutions onto the grid.

When determining whether users have asked for a solution, dig deeper to ascertain their awareness of the problem. Then work on understanding how well your solution actually solves that problem. Knowing and comparing both of these pieces of data is essential for you to understand how well a solution is performing.

If users say, 'Our highest priority is being able to collaborate with our existing tool,' do not blindly rush out to build multiuser support for them. Instead, find out *why* they think being able to collaborate on that tool is what they need. Is it genuinely the best way to solve their problem, or are they just so used to the tool that they haven't thought outside the box? Then build something that solves the problem in the most effective way, given time and budget constraints. Dig as deep as you can, explore their current solutions, and watch over their shoulder if possible. You may end up building exactly what they ask for, or you may gain some critical information that takes your solution in a whole new direction.

BUILD, MEASURE, ITERATE; ALWAYS

WHEN BUILDING A SOLUTION TO A PROBLEM, do not assume that you know exactly what needs to be built. Deeply embed yourself within the end users' experience to understand the ins and outs of the issues they face.

Make sure that you understand the industry you are building for. Some in the development team of CamelCat Marketing made the mistake of believing they worked in the *tech* industry, not the *marketing* industry. The truth is that they worked in both, but by abdicating responsibility for understanding the ins and outs of the industry they built for, they created a situation where they could only accept product specifications from others, and assumed that success would come if they just followed instructions. Just a little industry knowledge would have made the prospect of liaising directly and regularly with clients and customers a standard part of their process.

You can still run with hunches, but when you do so you should involve users as early as possible to get feedback on proof of concept builds and early betas. The time spent setting up the additional process to loop in these individuals will more than pay for itself with the information you gain from them, especially if it suggests that you should double down on, or abandon, an idea.

Most of the time you will build something that is *kind of* useful, but not completely. This is to be expected—you will rarely be an expert in the field you are building for, or know all of the quirks of a particular company or group of users. If, when you put your solution in front of people, you discover that there is a misalignment, that is okay. It may just be that [Your] Vision ≠ [Their] Reality. Use their feedback to realign and understand where your assumptions fell short. Make some changes, invite them to give feedback on a new iteration, try again.

Cameron worked in a silo, kept odd hours, and eschewed iterative feedback and testing loops, causing Project Accelerate to almost fail. In contrast, Alice encouraged collaborative working with open lines of communication, allowing the project first to pivot, then to iterate, until it reached a passable level.

This approach does not have to stop when the solution has been released. Things will change over time: markets will shift; competitors will disrupt the industry with new innovations that make your formerly perfect solution look terribly outdated; users will find themselves with new responsibilities that require them to do 10% of the job outside of your solution, then 20%, then 50%, until they reach a point where they have put the problem out to tender again, and you are one of many solution providers vying for the job.

If you do not keep up with what is changing in the world (or at least the industry you are building for), complacency will gradually erode your Mission Critical solution into something that is a veritable Waste of Time.

Never stop learning and iterating.

AIM TO SUCCEED OR FAIL

EVERYTHING YOU BUILD SHOULD HAVE the end goal of becoming either a Mission Critical solution, or an acknowledged Waste of Time.

In an ideal world, the things you build will be either:

- A fully formed Mission Critical solution;
- A Stroke of Genius that gains widespread acceptance and adoption to the point it becomes Mission Critical;
- A poor-performing example of where Vision ≠ Reality, which is improved upon until it becomes a usable, Mission Critical solution, or;
- An implementation so incredibly off the mark that it is a pure Waste of Time which, through intensive, iterative work gains realignment to something Mission Critical for users.

Ideally, every path leads to a high-demand/high-usage solution. But that is not the only acceptable outcome.

The things you build can also be either:

- An example of CV-driven development that serves no practical purpose and is recognised as a Waste of Time;
- An execution where Vision ≠ Reality because it has been driven by the solution's buyer rather than those who will be using it, and due to time constraints fails as a Waste of Time that cannot be reworked;
- A true Stroke of Genius that is too disruptive, and you do not have the resources or staying power to change perceptions to see widespread adoption, so instead becomes a Waste of Time that suffered for being ahead of its time, or;
- A celebrated Mission Critical solution for which you did not have the resources or organisational will required to play *keep up*, and over time becomes an unused, unwanted relic—a Waste of Time.

All of which you eventually have to gain the courage to kill.

A solution that lands anywhere on the grid can end up as a Waste of Time. If you do not have the will or resources to make a positive change, you must face the prospect of calling it a day, and burning down the castle.

COMMON SENSE SHOULD PREVAIL

ABOVE ALL ELSE, use your common sense. No model, framework, or self-help book will serve you perfectly, and this one is no exception.

You are likely working on projects that are fluid; that have been commissioned by people who are not really sure what they need. That is *why* they have commissioned you to build something for them.

So be receptive to things changing and your assumptions being flipped on their head. Augment your intuition and experience with tools such as this one, but do not assume that following them to the letter will lead you to success. You have to be an active participant in the process and use your common sense.

DON'T BE AFRAID TO MAKE TOUGH CHOICES

FINALLY, do not be afraid to recognise efforts that have been, in hindsight, a Waste of Time. Especially the big ones. Admit to them, ensure that you and you peers learn from them, and then allow yourself to at least take a morbid pleasure in burning down the castle.

GLOSSARY

1:1
A regular meeting where an individual and their manager discuss matters such as goals, blockers, feedback, and career progression. Agenda items are often set by the individual rather than the manager.

A/B Testing
A method of testing a potential improvement to a product or service, by continuing to serve the old solution alongside the new one, and measuring the effectiveness of each.

Alpha Testing
A form of pre-release testing, typically carried out within the organisation, often by those who are building the solution.

Application Programming Interface (API)
A public interface that allows a piece of software to receive and respond to external requests; in modern systems often made available over HTTP.

Basic Access Authentication (Basic Auth)
A method of authenticating a HTTP request, by passing a username/password combination to the server, typically as a Base64-encoded value in a header.

Beta Testing
A form of pre-release testing, typically carried out externally to the organisation, often by those for whom the solution is being built.

Blue Screen Of Death
A full-screen error message signifying that a fatal, unrecoverable error has occurred. Typically used by the Microsoft Windows operating system, and gaining notoriety in the 1990s.

Business-to-Consumer (B2C)
A business model where businesses deal with, and sell directly to, the consumer, bypassing the traditional distribution channels that may exist in their industry (e.g. third-party retail stores).

Cassette (Video/Audio)
A storage medium popular in the latter half of the 20th century, which used magnetic tapes to record and play back video and audio tracks. Used both for computing and home media purposes.

Comma-Separated Values (CSV)
A file format that represents tabulated data, where lines represent rows, and commas represent the division between columns. The values in the first row of a CSV file typically represent the names of the columns.

Content Delivery Network (CDN)

A network of servers, often distributed globally, from which web assets and HTTP requests are served to increase the availability and responsiveness of web sites and services.

Content Management System (CMS)

An application (often web-based) that facilitates the easy creation and maintenance of digital content such as web pages.

Continuous Integration / Continuous Delivery (CI/CD)

A software development practice where software built by disparate team members is reconciled on a regular basis, built, tested, and prepared for release. Often performed automatically when new code is pushed to a central repository. Automated code deployments are less common, but may be permitted if a number checks pass during the *integration* stage.

Conversion Rate

The rate at which a website guest converts into a customer by completing a transaction, such as placing an order. Typically, only a small percentage of guests will convert into customers.

Customer Relationship Management (CRM)

A technology (often web-based) that manages customer details and the organisation's interactions with them. The information stored in a CRM may be used by salespeople to help convert leads into paying customers.

CV-Driven Development (CDD)

The practice of deciding to implement specific technologies and processes based on the perceived value they will add to the CV (résumé) of those who implement or use them, rather than the actual value they will add to the project(s) in which they are used.

Database Management System (DBMS)

Software that allows users and applications to interact with a database storage layer by providing the means to query, manipulate, and analyse the stored data.

Decision Tree

A decision-making mechanism (often a portrayed as a flowchart-like diagram) that shows the possible decisions that can be made based on various conditions and criteria.

Direct Message (DM)

An electronic message sent directly from one individual to another, not visible to other users of the same platform. Often sent via a *chat* or *instant messaging* platform.

Floppy Disk

A computer storage medium popular in the latter half of the 20th century, which used magnetic disks to store and retrieve data. Typically capable of storing several hundred kilobytes of data.

Franking

The process of adding a franking mark (a pre-paid, printed stamp) to a letter or parcel.

grep

A UNIX utility that facilitates searching within plain-text data for lines that match a regular expression. When used as a verb, often refers to the act of searching for a value within a large set of data, such as application logs.

Integrated Development Environment (IDE)

A software application designed to aid software developers in the process of writing code. Differentiated from code editors by advanced functionality, such as compiling, debugging, and general task automation.

Integration Hell

The name given to the difficulty that arises when merging together the work carried out by multiple developers on a single codebase, especially when a significant amount of time has passed since the last integration, or when one or more pieces of work introduce significant changes to core parts of the codebase.

Machine Learning (ML)

The science of training computers to identify patterns in data, and to make predictions based on those patterns, without providing explicit instructions on how to solve specific problems.

Minimum Viable Product (MVP)

A version of a product or system that contains the bare minimum of functionality required to solve a problem, often to quickly get a solution into users' hands for the purpose of gathering feedback. An MVP may not contain advanced functionality, and may not be particularly easy to use.

Mechanical Turk (MTurk)

A black-box machine (named after a famous chess-playing 'machine' from the 1700s) that appears to contain advanced technology, but is in fact secretly operated by humans. In modern usage, normally refers to Amazon Mechanical Turk; a human crowdsourcing platform to which work can be requested via API.

Network-Attached Storage (NAS)

A computer storage device that is attached to a local network. It is accessible to other devices on the network as a shared drive or file-system mount.

OAuth

A protocol used for authenticating access to an application. Designed to allow users to log into an application using either a local account or a third-party account (e.g. a social media account). Upon successful authentication, provides an access token which can be used to authenticate subsequent requests to the application for the duration of the session.

Pay As You Go (PAYG)

A payment model where a product or service is paid for based on actual usage, as opposed to a fixed amount upfront.

Proof Of Concept (POC)

A simple execution of an idea, used to validate the fundamentals of the underlying premise. Proof-of-concept executions are generally disposed of once they have run their course. In some cases they are erroneously treated as MVPs and built upon, resulting in unnecessary technical debt.

Role-Based Access Control (RBAC)

A security model used to limit access to a system's resources, based on a user's role(s), as opposed to their identity. For example: a user with the *billing* role would be able to access payment details and invoices, whereas a user with only the *writer* role would not.

Schrödinger's Cat

A thought experiment used to illustrate the concept of superposition in quantum mechanics. The experiment posits that a cat placed inside a closed box with a vial of poison that is released by a random event (such as the decay of a radioactive atom) can be considered simultaneously dead and alive, until such time as the box is opened and the state of the cat is observed.

Single Pane Of Glass

A tool that combines data or information from multiple disparate sources into a single, unified presentation layer (the so-called *single pane of glass*).

Software House

A company that produces software for its clients.

Sunk-Cost Fallacy

The phenomenon where an individual or group will continue to sink time, effort, money, or some other resource into a project or endeavour that is no longer yielding a positive net result, out of a reluctance to admit failure or defeat.

The Great Gig In The Sky
The final song on Side One of the 1973 Pink Floyd album *The Dark Side of the Moon*. The song is known for its soaring, emotive vocal performance.

Training Bias
Deviations from reality that occur in the output of machine learning models resulting from overweighted or overrepresented elements in the dataset used to train them.

User Acceptance Testing (UAT)
A form of pre-release testing, carried out by those for whom the solution has been built, ideally in real-world scenarios. Often the final stage of testing prior to release.

User Experience (UX)
The experience a user has when interacting with a product or service, especially as it relates to design, accessibility, and the ease with which the solution solves the user's problem(s).

Video Cassette Recorder (VCR)
A device used to play from and record onto video cassette tapes. Ubiquitous in homes during the 1980s and 1990s, enabling consumers to easily record television shows.

What You See Is What You Get (WYSIWYG)
An approach to content editing that provides the ability to update content in situ, or in a manner that otherwise displays to the editor the look and feel the content will take on once it has been published. Typically pronounced *wizzy-wig*.

ACKNOWLEDGEMENTS

I would like to thank Shelley, who has not only put up with me while I wrote another book, but has contributed the character illustrations that help bring the parable to life.

Thank you to my former colleagues Caleb Ndlovu and Simon Jones for acting as a sounding board when I first began to articulate this idea, and for offering challenges and insights along the way.

And a big thank you to those who helped me to learn and iterate on this book by volunteering their time to proofread and feed back on it: Daniel Tallentire, Mike Reidy, Jason Crome, and Cristian Caratti.

In gaining feedback, I have been faced with tough decisions about the structure of the book, and it has been a stark reminder that, even when you speak to end users, they will not all feel the same way. By finding common themes in feedback, I have been able to make informed decisions about how much to change, and in what ways.

ABOUT THE AUTHOR

David Maidment is a technologist residing in the United Kingdom. He is a software engineer of thirty years, and since 2019 has run the Software Engineering departments of edtech and fintech companies.

He is a keen mentor, helping students and others new to the industry navigate the challenge of getting their first tech job, and thereafter growing as professionals.

As a public speaker, he appears as a guest on webinars and podcasts, and speaks at tech events, often on the subjects of *paths into tech*, *digital transformation*, and *useless software*—the last of which he enjoys creating to keep his programming skills sharp.

ALSO BY DAVID MAIDMENT

Becoming Management

Printed in Great Britain
by Amazon

25575780R00129